QUEEN OF PARADOX

MARY STUART, QUEEN OF SCOTS

QUEEN OF PARADOX

A STUART TRAGEDY

by Katherine Brégy

"... *The most gracious, courteous royal lady*
That ever was betrayed by brutal men
And greedy men, and scoundrels and base knaves,
Falsehood and savagery and forgery."

John Masefield (*End and Beginning*)

THE BRUCE PUBLISHING COMPANY • MILWAUKEE

10, 13p

92
Mar 9
Stu
Re 49

TO

MARY

HERSELF

RECONNAISSANCES

T HE author tenders thanks for counsel or encouragement or the loan of rare books to the Very Reverend Robert I. Gannon, S.J.; the Right Reverend Edward Hawks, the Reverend Philip E. Donahue and the Reverend James A. Magner, Ph.D.; to Mother Mary Lawrence of Rosemont College and Professor Conyers Read of the University of Pennsylvania; to Commander R. Langton-Jones, R.N.R.; to Miss Maria Steuart of Edinburgh and Ethel Tate McKenzie; to Julie Kernan and Theodore Maynard; to the Libraries of the University of Pennsylvania and the Saint Andrew's Society of Philadelphia and the Free Libraries of Philadelphia and New York City. Especially is she indebted to her sister, Edith M. Brégy, for her heartening interest throughout the writing of the book and to Virginia L. Martin for her patient devotion and efficiency in typing the entire manuscript.

Acknowledgment is also given to the Macmillan Company for kind permission to quote from John Masefield's poem, "End and Beginning."

QUEEN OF PARADOX: A STUART TRAGEDY

DRAMATIS PERSONAE

MARY STUART — Queen of Scotland: born 1542, died 1587

JAMES V, KING OF SCOTLAND — father of Mary Stuart: son of James IV of Scotland and Margaret Tudor (daughter of Henry VII and sister of Henry VIII of England)

MARIE DE GUISE — mother of Mary Stuart: wife and queen of James V: sister of François, Duke of Guise and Charles, Cardinal of Lorraine

DAVID, CARDINAL BEATON — Archbishop of St. Andrews: adviser to Marie de Guise until his murder in 1546

LORD JAMES STUART — natural son of James V and brother of Mary: later Earl of Moray

JOHN KNOX — preacher and head of the Protestant Scottish Kirk

JAMES, EARL OF ARRAN (later Duke of Châtelheraut) — head of the Hamilton clan: first Regent for Mary Stuart: father of the younger, half-mad Earl of Arran (also James), and of Lord Claude Hamilton

HENRY STUART, LORD DARNLEY — son of the Earl and Countess of Lennox: second husband of Mary Stuart: assassinated 1567

JAMES VI OF SCOTLAND — son of Mary and Darnley: later King James I of England

HENRI II — King of France

CATHERINE DE MEDICI — his wife and queen

FRANÇOIS II — their eldest son: first husband of Mary Stuart. His brothers include the future Charles IX, Henri III, and the Duke of Anjou

HENRY VIII — King of England: uncle of James V

EDWARD VI — his son by Jane Seymour

MARY TUDOR — Queen of England: Henry's daughter by Catherine of Aragon

ELIZABETH — Queen of England: his daughter by Anne Boleyn

WILLIAM CECIL, LORD BURGHLEY — Elizabeth's Lord Treasurer and "Power behind the Throne"

SIR FRANCIS WALSINGHAM — Secretary of State under Cecil and head of Elizabethan Secret Service

SIR WILLIAM MAITLAND OF LETHINGTON — Mary Stuart's Secretary of State

JAMES DOUGLAS, EARL OF MORTON — Mary's Chancellor after Huntley's death

JOHN ERSKINE, EARL OF MAR (restored to this title when Lord James Stuart became Earl of Moray) — Guardian of Edinburgh Castle and of the infant James VI

DAVID RIZZIO — Italian musician and secretary to Mary Stuart: assassinated in 1566

GEORGE, EARL OF HUNTLEY — leader of the Gordon Highlanders: Chancellor of Scotland: dispossessed by Mary, who later restored his son, Lord George Gordon, to her favor and his father's title

JAMES HEPBURN, EARL OF BOTHWELL — Grand Admiral of Scotland: later Duke of Orkney: third husband of Mary Stuart

MARY SEATON, MARY BEATON, MARY FLEMING, and MARY LIVINGSTON: lifelong attendants upon Mary Stuart: later joined by JANE KENNEDY

BOURGOYNE — Mary's faithful physician during her imprisonment

CLAUDE NAU — her French secretary

GILBERT CURLL — her Scottish secretary

GILBERT GIFFORD — an English spy who engineered the Babington Plot

ANTHONY BABINGTON — an English gentleman and champion of Mary Stuart: executed for participation in plot bearing his name

Among the many *Ambassadors,* the principal names to be remembered are: on the English side, *Sadler, Throckmorton,* and *Randolph;* on the French *du Croc, de la Mauvissière,* and *de Chateauneuf;* and Mary Stuart's own representatives *Sir James Melville, John Leslie* the *Bishop of Ross,* and *James Beaton* the *Bishop of Glasgow.*

FOREWORD: OF PARADOX

THE story of Mary Stuart is a kind of microcosm not merely of the universal paradox of humanity but also of the special paradoxes of her age. It was the age of the so-called Reformation, when evil and good, greed and idealism, politics and religion became almost hopelessly entangled: a hard age to see straight in, as even St. Thomas More found. The life span of Mary Stuart covered the most extreme contrasts, touching that of Henry VIII and Ignatius Loyola, of Philip II and Don John of Austria, of Catherine de Medici and John Knox, of the aging Elizabeth and the young Shakespeare. The tragically delayed Council of Trent began its epochal work of clarifying dogma and correcting ecclesiastical abuses in 1545, three years after Mary's birth — when it was finally dissolved in 1563 the Counter-Reformation had become a reality.

And like all ages when men's religious beliefs have been violently shaken, their spiritual and material values rendered insecure, it fell prey to all sorts of hysterical excesses. Both national and international morality were at a low ebb, the questionable doctrine of regicide being only discouraged by the equally questionable one of the "divine right" of kings. As the old ideal of Christendom faded, nationalism grew apace. And the newest of private sects were as eager to entrench themselves as State religions, and to persecute anyone opposing their authority, as the ancient and embattled Catholic Church. The time was full of genius and perversity, of courage and hypocrisy, when the subtle simplicities of the Ages of Faith met headlong the adventurous egotism, the art, the passionate but not yet frank materialism of the Renaissance. As Mr. D. J. Wyndham Lewis points out in discussing the poet Ronsard, it was an age of "immense wickedness, immense beauty, immense learning, and — it seems time it was mentioned — immense goodness."

The Queen of Scots was conditioned by her background and her surroundings — "even as you and I." She was a very human and most of the time a rather lonely woman: more than usually beautiful, more than usually magnetic, proud and sensitive, scholarly and sympathetic, a lover of fine books and fine clothes, a lover of love and fair play. She was centuries ahead of her age in toleration, always intelligent in her Faith, and as years wore on devout to the point of martyrdom. With little physical resistance and some neuroticism, she could call upon terrific reserves of will and of feminine endurance. She was also trustful to a fault and an incredibly poor judge of men. As overcivilized and imprudent queen of a turbulent and uncivilized country — again as Catholic heir to the throne of a Protestant England — she was the inevitable target of jealousy, treachery, and persecution, predestined on the human side to failure and heartbreak. Potentially, perhaps even actually, both sinner and saint, Mary remains one of the most fascinating problems in all history.

K. B.

CONTENTS

QUEEN OF PARADOX

CHAPTER I

CRADLE AND CROWN

MARY STUART was nine months old and had just been crowned Queen of Scotland and the Isles. Lawful Queen she had been, indeed, since the first week of her life, when her luckless father James V had died because he no longer wished to live after his defeat by the English at Solway Moss. But it was not until this 9th of September, 1543 — precisely thirty years after the unforgotten, unforgiven debacle of Flodden Field — that the infant was actually consecrated in the chapel of Stirling Castle.

Marie of Guise, her gallant French mother, had prayed and fought and maneuvered for the day, aided chiefly by the one friend she could trust in all Scotland, that Cardinal Beaton standing now before the candlelit altar. With anxious concentration she watched the baby lying so quietly in the arms of Stirling's Lord Keeper, dozing through most of the ceremony, but waking to whimper a little when the heavy Scottish crown was pressed against her forehead: the crown which her father had made heavier when he added two golden arches with globe and cross to the simpler jewelled band of his forefathers. The tall Queen Mother was wise and foreseeing, but luckily not even she could suspect how soon she must lose her fearless guide, the

1

Cardinal, by assassination, nor could plumb the sinister roles to be played in her daughter's life by the three lairds of the realm standing closest beside her. First came James Hamilton, the shifty Earl of Arran—acting Regent and, through his Stuart grandmother, next in line to the throne; and so privileged to carry that crown which he and his half-mad son were to covet and endanger. Next stood George, Fourth Earl of Huntley, proud head of the Gordon clan and "cock o' the north," bearing the beautiful Italian sword of State — a gift from Pope Julius II to James IV when the latter was named Defender of the Faith — which the young Queen was so unwisely to turn against him. And ironically enough, the scepter, with its tiny statues of our Lady, St. Andrew, and St. James, was held by the Earl of Lennox — soon to be banished to England for treason, and there to become father of the boy who was to blacken history as Mary's traitor husband, Lord Darnley.

The little procession filed out of the chapel and back to the royal apartments, where the infant could be unbundled from her cloth of gold and laid gently in her cradle. She had recently come through a slight attack of smallpox — scourge in those ages of rich and poor, high and low — but was essentially sound and beautiful: "as goodly a child as I have seen of her age, and as like to live, with the grace of God," the English Ambassador had reported when the Queen Mother allowed the baby to be stripped in his presence to silence rumors of her ill-health. Marie of Guise, still young, still fair herself, presided ceremoniously at the health-drinking, kissed the Cardinal's ring, and slipped back to watch beside her child, while the faithful nurse Janet Sinclair chatted quietly with some ladies-in-waiting at the far end of the chamber. It had been a kind of *sub rosa* coronation: a march stolen upon the jealous Scottish barons already murmuring against a woman ruler, and upon Henry of

England, already seeking the baby girl as future bride for his sickly six-year-old son, Edward.

Marie raised her head a little higher at the thought of English Harry. A few years before, when death had taken both her own young husband, the Duke of Longuéville, and Henry's Jane Seymour, he who was to be dubbed the British Bluebeard came seeking herself for his fourth mate. And she, Catholic daughter of the mighty house of Guise, had refused to become precarious Queen of a schismatic England. But when James of Scotland, mourning the loss of his first wife, the French princess, Marguerite, had begged her hand — largely, perhaps, to continue the friendly pact between their two countries — she acceded willingly enough. It was not easy to leave her little son François and the close ties of the great Guise family, nor to go to a land she knew to be cold and half-civilized beside her own. But she was schooled already in the discipline which identified duty with statecraft. And this auburn-haired, reckless Scotch husband was a winsome fellow, even if there seemed almost as little chance of being his first love as his last. She knew the wound of losing his frail French Marguerite was scarcely healed. Earlier there must have been another wound when he could not wed young Margaret Erskine, bride instead of his enemy Douglas, who had nonetheless given him the sly-faced silent son known as Lord James Stuart. Others there had been and still might be, but the wise Gallic widow cared not too much about those light loves. In her youthful chief of a fierce and feudal country there was a bluff fascination for this daughter of sophisticated France. James moved jovially among his people — even the bitter-tongued Knox was later to acknowledge him "a good poor man's king" — and she knew that in spite of self-will and weakness of the flesh he would keep the Faith. Had he not given the perfect answer when Henry VIII's ambassador, the wily Sadler, had suggested that he, too, might pardonably liquidate Church revenues since certain of the Scottish Orders had stumbled into abuse? "God forbid that, if a few be not good, for them all the rest should be destroyed," the Stuart replied with unanswerable simplicity. Marie had loved that blending of good sense and good will. So it was as a helpmate in all ways that she came to him; encouraging his love of music and the other arts, even sending back to France for trained masons and miners to develop his country's resources.

It seemed bitter payment that the two baby sons she bore him had died within a week. And just when this third child was expected there had come one of the perennial English raids across the Border, a sally long enough to destroy the hard-won Scottish harvest. By November her own King set out to avenge the outrage with his ill-prepared band of peasants, Church retainers, and undisciplined nobles. . . . Why must men always be fighting for one cause or another? Tears came into the eyes of the widowed Queen as she recalled that last defeat which had broken the spirit and cost the life of her husband. He was thirty-two, but he had no will to carry on: he had not even cared to see the baby daughter she had brought into the world that bleak December night at Linlithgow Castle. For he did not want a daughter. "It came with a lass and it will go with a lass," the messenger told her he had cried out half-deliriously, quoting some ancient Scotch prophecy about the Stuart kingdom.

Not if she, this lass's mother, could hold it fast for her against the treachery of jealous lords and the violence of fast-increasing heretics at home, or the menace of that "Auld Inimy" across the Border. Marie crossed herself and knelt beside the baby's cradle, praying silently. Then, opening her eyes, she found herself gazing straight into the eyes of the half-awakened infant — Stuart eyes, dark hazel, long, and deep-set, below the auburn Stuart hair. And up into her mother's face Queen Mary sent the irresistible Stuart smile.

Marie de Guise smiled back. Not even the most evil-minded of her enemies could deny the child's legitimacy, at any rate, which was something in this land of calumny and confusion. The young eyes closed again drowsily, but in the mother's heart remained a sense of awe and wonder and misgiving. From some corner of her memory floated back the prophecy spoken of another, greater Baby: *This Child is set for the fall and rising again of many . . . and for a sign that shall be spoken against. . . .* Again she crossed herself. What prodigious destiny hovered above the tiny girl who asked only a little security and peace? Was she to be a saint or a sinner — or like most of us, something of both? A *queen* in any case: upon that her mother was determined. Royally she should walk through life and into death.

The woman rose from her knees, signalled quietly to Janet Sinclair, and walked over to the narrow window, drawing back the tapestry and gazing out into the darkening autumn night. High above Stirling Castle, that old fortress perched upon steep rocks at the gateway of the Highlands, wind clouds seemed bent upon puffing out the stars. A storm was gathering over Scotland. But Scotland was used to storms.

CHAPTER   II

MOTHER AND CHILD AGAINST THE WORLD

M<small>ARIE OF GUISE</small> had seen her share of storm clouds, too. France, as she now looked back upon the days of her girlhood and her girlhood's marriage, seemed a garden spot of peace. Yet there had always been a battle getting won or lost: a battle in which her brother, the masterful Duke of Guise, was at the forefront, just as her younger brother, the Cardinal of Lorraine, was now at the forefront against the Huguenot uprisings fast taking on the proportions of civil war. She was a woman of peace herself — more tolerant even of religious differences than would have met the approval of her adamantine family — born into a warring world of which Scotland seemed the bristling outpost.

James V was scarcely in his tomb when the governing council named in his deathbed will — Cardinal Beaton and the Earls of Moray and Argyle, with herself in charge of the infant Queen — had been superseded by the Earl of Arran, whose claims of precedence were admitted by a nobility united only in its dual suspicion of clerics and women. She had seen her faithful Cardinal imprisoned in the castle of Blackness, and had been helpless to prevent the venal Arran and his Parliament from accepting Henry VIII's proposal that her baby daughter be immediately betrothed to little

Prince Edward, and delivered over to the English "before she be ten years old at the farthest." It was generally understood that Arran, as a reward for this complicity, had been promised the hand of the Princess Elizabeth — whom Henry had, however, declared illegitimate a few years before! — for his own eldest son. But the English tyrant had a way of defeating himself by overreaching: and when he promptly demanded that Stirling Castle, along with Dumbarton, St. Andrews, and a few other strongholds be handed over to his garrisons, and all treaties with France abrogated, his pattern for the total subjugation of Scotland became evident to everybody. It was then that his ambassador at Edinburgh, the notorious Sadler, wrote back to the King his impressions that not only were "all the clergy" and "many noblemen" (all, that is to say, still uncorrupted by English bribes) against such measures, but that "If we prepare to bring the obedience of this realm to the King of England there is not so little a boy but he will hurl stones against it, the wives will handle their distaffs and the commons will rather die than submit to it." So the voice of the people, including the voice of the women, prevailed as it always does when resolutely raised. Arran yielded sufficiently to permit Cardinal Beaton to return to his northern see of St. Andrews. He even disavowed his recent Protestant conversion and was temporarily reconciled to the Church he had repudiated. The Queen Mother and her child were removed to the greater security of Stirling Castle, where the moral and tactical victory of the coronation became a fact.

For Marie de Guise and the Cardinal and even the weathercock Arran knew that, as soon as the merciful hardness of the Scotch winter was over, Henry would strike back in revenge for this thwarting of his will and his pride. Already the Queen Mother had begged help from her own fatherland, and during that autumn of 1543 a few French ships had sailed into Leith carrying supplies — and incidently carrying the Papal envoy Grimaldi, with instructions to report upon conditions of the Scottish Church and State. These impressions were far from encouraging, as he warned the parliament at Edinburgh before returning to France.

But no one was prepared for the scope and savagery of the English attack which began in May, 1544, when more than two hundred vessels flaunting Henry's banners suddenly appeared in the harbors of Leith and Edinburgh, while the land was overrun by English troops. We know now exactly what instructions the Earl of Hertford, leading the invasion, had been given for his treatment of Scotland: "His Majesty's pleasure is that you put all to fire and sword, burn Edinburgh town, let it be so razed and defaced when you have sacked and gotten what you can of it, as there may remain a perpetual memory of the vengeance of God. . . . Do what ye can out of hand and without long tarrying to beat down and overthrow the Castle, sack Holyrood House and as many towns and villages about Edinburgh as ye may conveniently. Sack Leith . . . putting man, woman and child to fire and sword without exception where any resistance should be made against you. This done, press over to the Fifeland and extend like extremities and destructions in all towns where ye may conveniently reach, not forgetting among the rest so to spoil and turn upside down the Cardinal's town of St. Andrews, as the upper stone may be the nether . . . sparing no creature alive within the same, especially such as, either in friendship or blood, be allied to the Cardinal." As an afterthought of propaganda, placards were to be placed on the ruins warning people they might "thank their Cardinal therefor," which Henry suggested might be "a good and grave device to cause the realm to bear hatred unto him."

It was a typical outpouring of sadistic Tudor hate and hypocrisy, under which Scotland was mowed down almost as effectively as by our modern tanks and bombs. Yet as we moderns have reason to know, not even tanks and bombs can prevail permanently against the human will. For more than a year the raids continued: not only the men but their "wives and bairns" were burned in their homes, while hospitals, monasteries, and the beautiful abbeys of Melrose, Dryburgh, Jedburgh, and Kelso were destroyed: yet the indomitable Scotch fought on to protect their homeland and Queen, rallied and guided by their indomitable Cardinal Beaton.

Against the latter, as Hertford's order implied, Henry's fury was particularly vindictive. In him was symbolized both the nation and the Church the King was bent upon demolishing. So when it became evident that fire and sword might ravage without subduing Scotland—or without even securing the custody of the infant Queen he already considered his future daughter-in-law — the English King began to weigh more personal methods of what today might be called liquidation. There were plenty of potential Scotch assassins, even among the nobility — had not Kirkaldy of Grange and the Earls of Cassillis and Brunston already indicated their willingness to end the Cardinal's activities if sufficiently rewarded? But Scotch thrift had an inconvenient way of demanding payment before instead of after the criminal event. And Henry was wary of going on record with advance payments, as also of making Beaton a national martyr. He preferred — and evidently handed on the preference to his daughter Elizabeth — a veneer of justice upon his crimes. And being quite familiar with the religious differences already dividing Scotland, he was willing to wait. "In the meanwhile," we are told by Lord Herries, "those of the reformed religion consulted which way to cut down the Cardinal, that by his death the Reformers may have more freedom." Their clock struck twelve in the spring of 1546, when George Wishart, an itinerant Calvinist preacher suspected also of being supported by the English Henry, was convicted of heresy by an ecclesiastical court presided over by Beaton and — according to the blind but universal law of the times, which identified heresy with treason — put to death by the civil authorities. Two months later that standing conspiracy backed by the Reformers, Henry himself and the Scottish lords in his pay, reached its climax. Early on the morning of May 29th, a band of assassins headed by John and Norman Leslie and Kirkaldy of Grange broke into the Cardinal's bedroom and stabbed the defenseless churchman to death: after which the poor, insulted body was sacrilegiously clothed in his pontifical vestments and hung over the blockhouse wall for the edification of the populace. Then a rare company of rogues — including a young zealot named John Knox, who was later to describe the details of the murder "full merrily" — moved into St. Andrews Castle. For over a year they held the fortress against the authorities of Scotland, terrifying and looting the countryside, and receiving supplies from English ships sailing surreptitiously into St. Andrews harbor.

When it became obvious that the feeble efforts of Arran and his impoverished Scotch army were futile to regain this northern stronghold, Marie de Guise in desperation again besought her brothers and the French king to send assistance. At long last it came, and the summer of 1547 saw twenty-one galleys in the harbor, armed with artillery which opened fire when the garrison refused to yield. At the end of July, William Kirkaldy surrendered to the French admiral, and by unusual clemency the rebels were not put to death but taken back to France in the galleys. Among them was John Knox, who seems to have been a kind of self-appointed chaplain to the outfit — and who turned up before long as a preacher in the town of Berwick, England.

In January of that year 1547 Henry VIII had been called

to his final reckoning, leaving to the English throne his rather pitiful young son Edward VI. But this meant no surcease for Scotland, since the very Hertford who had directed her recent martyrdom now became Lord Protector or Regent with the title of Duke of Somerset. Once again the question of little Mary Stuart's marriage to Edward came up for discussion, and when Scotland again refused, Somerset promptly ordered a fresh invasion. His army is said to have been more then 30,000 strong (one can never be too sure of these reported figures) with a fleet of 65 ships patrolling the seacoast, for he had recently recalled large numbers of troops from service against France and Spain. In desperation Arran revived the ancient Scottish SOS of the Fiery Cross, which was carried through Highlands and Lowlands calling upon the services of all men between sixteen and sixty years old. Like most Scotch armies, they were brave but undisciplined and unused to acting in concert. So there came upon Scotland the formidable and almost fatal defeat of Pinkie Cleugh, in which some fourteen thousand of her sons became corpses before the English army retired across the Border for supplies. "It was a famous victory" — but as usual, nothing lasting had been accomplished.

In this bleak hour the child Queen — innocent heart of all these turbulent currents of ambition and revenge, loyalty, treason, and mourning — was sent by her mother for safety to the island monastery of Inchmahome in the Highlands, where Lord Erskine's son John was prior. With her went Janet Sinclair, the latter's husband John Kemp of the Royal Guards, and the four little companions who were to be with her through so much joy and sorrow: her cousin Mary Fleming; Mary Beaton, niece of the murdered Cardinal; Mary Livingston; and Mary Seaton. "Isle of Rest" was the meaning of the island's name; and here through the winter the children found peaceful shelter, continuing their lessons under the monks' care, and when spring came learning about the well-kept gardens and familiar birds. Here for the first time Mary Stuart had her own plot of flowers to tend; and the box hedge outlining her tiny garden is still pointed out, although the monastery has been for centuries in ruins.

But Marie of Guise knew there must be a more distant and definite refuge for her child, and added enormously to her prestige by securing it through her own family. By tact and persistence she won the consent of the Scottish Estates — already united by recent events in their antipathy to England — to the Queen's betrothal to the young French Dauphin, son of Henri II, with her immediate removal to France for education. And to make sure of Arran, whom she well described as "the most inconstant man in the world," she captured for him the French dukedom of Châtelheraut.

So in the summer of 1548 a new and smaller fleet of French galleys under Admiral Villegaignon eluded the spying ships of Somerset, and by a skillful feat of seamanship sailed around the north of Scotland and secretly into the Firth of Clyde. The already lovely little Queen — not quite six years old — was waiting at Dumbarton, and with the small train, including her aunt Lady Fleming and the flock of Marys, was welcomed honorably by the Sieur de Brézé and quietly packed on board. From the desolate Scotch coast her mother watched alone that August day, as all she loved best on earth set out upon the precarious voyage to the land she loved best, too. It would have been easy to persuade herself that she was needed to accompany her royal child, and that the lords of Scotland could be left for a few years to their own wranglings. But Marie of Guise was not given to choosing the easiest way.

CHAPTER III

A GIRL AT WORK AND PLAY

LATER on, a tiny Gothic chapel dedicated to the Scotch saint, Ninian, was raised at Roscoff on the Breton coast to mark the spot where Mary Stuart first set her foot on French soil — or as it happened, on the French rocks. Her party, half French, half Scotch, arrived after more than a week's stormy voyaging, which the royal child seems to have weathered better than her elders. In fact, one of the earliest of Mary's really personal reactions to come down to us is the story of her teasing her pretty aunt, Lady Fleming, about being wretchedly seasick!

Now from far and near came sailors and fishermen and peasants to greet the little girl they had been told was to be their future Queen; and if she could not always understand their speech they could all understand her smile. Soon the journey became a kind of triumphal march, in which the child's litter was preceded by gaily caparisoned horsemen and followed by great coaches lent by the King of France. In the church of Notre Dame at Morlaix a *Te Deum* was sung in thanksgiving for her safe arrival. At Nantes a company of 150 small boys dressed in white satin greeted her with military maneuvers, accompanied by a juvenile band. Then came the leisurely boat journey on the Loire in the gentle September sunshine. This meant passing through one of the garden spots of France, its natural beauty freshly pointed by the exquisitely modeled châteaux which had replaced the old fortress-homes of the French nobles and their kings. And to the Scottish children and their elders, used to a harsh land where even the violet of thistle or heather was too often trampled and blood-stained by invading armies, it must have seemed a dream stolen from fairyland.

Now, too, little Mary began meeting her mother's illustrious family, about whom she had heard much and whose influence she was to feel more and more powerfully. First came her maternal grandfather, the veteran soldier Claude de Guise, with his devout and devoted wife, Antoinette de Bourbon. Next the awed but apparently never overawed child was presented to her uncle the mighty Duc François de Guise, that warrior to whom France was to owe both Metz and Calais — and to his younger brother Charles, the Cardinal of Lorraine, leader of the French Church in its growing warfare against the Huguenots, and almost immediately self-appointed mentor of Mary's own educational process. She met also, and happily, her French half brother, the young Duc de Longuéville. And at Carrières came the first momentous encounter with her fiancé François, a frail child of slight energy who promptly adored the healthy little Scotch girl. The Dauphin was not quite five years old, but children in those days were dressed and apparently treated as much as possible like small editions of their elders: so when the Venetian ambassador, Capello, recorded that the boy already "showed that he knew himself a prince," it probably meant nothing very alarming. Equally serious and rather more significant was a message written to one of the Guise household in October by King Henri II: "My daughter the Queen of Scotland arrived Sunday in very good health at Carrières, where my own children are. From the letters from . . . your mother and my cousin the Sieur d'Humières, my son and she were from the first day as great chums as though they had long known each other. No one comes near her without marvellous praise — which redoubles my own wish to see her." When they did meet at Saint-Germain-en-Laye a few weeks later, Mary's conquest of the still youthful monarch was complete. He had already given orders that, as a crowned Queen, she should be given official precedence over his little sons and daughters: now he described her as "the most perfect child I ever knew." For alas! his own brood by the unloved and unlovely Catherine de Medici left much to be desired.

As everybody at court and in Europe knew, Henri's heart had long ago been given to a woman twenty years his senior — Diane de Poitiers, Duchesse de Valentinois, who had so strangely charmed his father, François I, also. This enigmatic widow bore scant resemblance to any usual picture of the royal mistress. Dressed perpetually in half mourning — which became her as well as Electra! — she was not overwhelmingly beautiful, but quite notably gracious, discreet, and economical; urging the King to reduce extravagances handed on from his father, interesting herself in the education of his children, and encouraging him in all duties to his Florentine wife — except the difficult duty of faithfulness and the impossible one of love.

Queen Catherine was rather a pitiful figure in those days, although later on she became a sinister one. She had been only fourteen when she came as a bride to France, and the first ten years of her marriage were ominously sterile — after which she bore ten children in quick succession. She was art-loving and book-loving, tactful, patient, and inscrutable. Heiress of the decadent but still dominant Medici family and niece of Pope Clement VII, she knew herself spoken of in France as a "money-lender's daughter," and her piety was always — and rightly — suspect. So a festering inferiority complex developed, which in the future was to work itself out in tyranny and cruelty. Something in her nature may well have turned sour as she watched those flauntingly interwined initials — always *H* and *D!* — on palace frescoes; and it was not sweetened even when Diane risked her life to nurse the Queen through a malignant fever. Like many frustrated people without much real faith, Catherine was highly superstitious and given to explorations in magic. She had a tower built for her official astrologer, and apparently it was she who first put the prophetic Nostradamus on the map. One day in the future this embittered woman, turning to power politics from the faith she had lost hold of and the love she had never won, was to write her autograph in blood across the feast of St. Bartholomew!

Both Catherine and Diane were knowing enough to recognize the growing charm of the "reinette," Mary: the Queen with secret jealousy — although she wrote enthusiastic congratulations to Marie de Guise upon her daughter — the royal favorite with motherly solicitude and that prudence which so many imprudent women love and foster in the younger generation. It was one of life's ironies that the Queen of Scots should have become the innocent means of hurting and humiliating Diane de Poitiers, when her fair but frivolous aunt, Lady Fleming (a natural sister of James V) temporarily lured the somewhat philandering King Henri into a new inconstancy — and got herself promptly banished from court.

Nobody could pretend, of course, that this court or any other was an ideal place for the upbringing of a child. It had the characteristic Renaissance mixture of faith and paganism, of culture, cruelty, and corruption. But it was a far better court than that of François I, which preceded it — or that of Catherine de Medici and her sons, which followed. The Sieur Jean d'Humières took very seriously his post as governor of the royal children (there were about thirty in all, including some of the high nobles' families), carefully directing their work and play if not always their diet. Over a hundred servants were in attendance; and there were competent instructors in Latin, Greek, religion, literature and composition, playing upon the harpsichord and other instruments, singing, the stately dancing of the times, and embroidery — all of which Mary mastered sufficiently to carry with her into the years ahead. And for playtime there were the friendly royal zoos to visit, and riding — Mary's own pet mares being named Bravane and Madame la Réale — or tennis and other games; while masque and pageants were the rage of the day.

The court itself was somewhat itinerant, and from time to time the children and their preceptors were moved *en masse* (it has been suggested for the practical purpose of housecleaning!) from St. Germain to Blois or Amboise, or even to Fontainebleau and Paris. Once for almost a year young Mary was taken from this whole worldly milieu by her grandmother — now putting into practice St. Paul's ideal of a Christian widow — and installed at the convent of Saint-Pierre-les-Dames near Rheims, presided over by her aunt, the Abbess Renée de Guise. She was happy there: dangerously happy in the opinion of her uncle the Cardinal of Lorraine. It was he — more statesman than churchman — who brought her back to court.

The visit of Marie de Guise during 1550–1551 was a warm joy to her little transplanted daughter. With the brutal Somerset superseded by the more temperate Warwick, and a general if ephemeral peace treaty in effect between England, France, and Scotland, the Queen Mother felt free at last to leave her discordant realm and see how things were going among her own people. She was royally received and entertained by Henri and Catherine: but when the matter of the financial and military help still urgently needed for Scotland came up, she found that kings are quicker to promise than to pay. There were other troubles during her year's stay: the mysterious attempted poisoning of the child Mary by a fanatical young Scottish Protestant who had been accepted as one of the attendants at the French court; and the death of her son by that happy first marriage, the young Duc de Longuéville. Nor were the conferences with her powerful brothers any too satisfactory. Neither the Duke of Guise nor the Cardinal seems to have gauged the acute danger and difficulty shadowing Marie's adopted throne — at root the same threat of civil and religious warfare rumbling through France, but accentuated by the feudal jealousies of the Scotch nobility, the particularly bitter brand of Scotch Protestantism and the insular Scotch resentment of all foreign influence. Marie de Guise both desired and determined to be named regent herself, in place of the unpopular Earl of Arran (Châtelheraut), but she had no intention of using a giant's power like a giant. Both by nature and experience she was all for conciliation. If before her death she made mistakes in policy, they were chiefly the results of French advice unsupported by French arms.

So when the Queen Mother sailed away from France in October, 1551, she carried with her the promise of the regency and the assurance of Mary's welfare and devotion, but not much else. She would be returning later on, of course, for her daughter's marriage! . . . Meanwhile, one hopes she took comfort in the cordial welcome given her at the English court, where she stayed a short while before passing on to Scotland. There was talk at this time of betrothing young Edward VI to the French King's daughter — Mary's devoted playmate, the little Madame Ysabel — and the nations were snatching a brief breathing space of peace.

It was a busy and a happy time for Mary Stuart, who,

now in her tenth year, seems to have acquired much of that magnetic and mysterious fascination which was to be hers to the end. This was a blend of piquancy and high seriousness, with Scotch independence adding tang to the grace of her French blood and education. She had an exquisite paleness of skin, deep heathery eyes which could look either blue or hazel, and red-brown Stuart hair. "When she grows I think she will be beautiful," her cautious grandmother had early prophesied, "for her hair is fine and her skin clear and white." And she added discerning comments upon Mary's deep-set eyes, her well-shaped face, above all her intelligence and the gracious self-assurance and poise "remarkable in one so young." By February, 1553, the Cardinal of Lorraine was assuring his sister that the girl Queen "improves daily in goodness and virtue, in beauty and intelligence. . . . She talks as well and as sensibly as if she were a woman of twenty-five": in proof of which he declared that "she rules both king and queen," Henri himself sometimes sitting down to converse with her as long as an hour! The delightfully gossipy Brantôme hands down the information that the royal girl managed somehow to look charming even when she appeared at court in an improvised and "savage" Highland costume, and spoke the "barbarous" tongue of her native Scotland in a manner *"très belle et très agréable."* And Madame Paroys, that chaperon of untiring virtue and vigilance who had succeeded the light-minded Lady Fleming, adds her somewhat prim testimony that Mary "gives pleasure to everyone who sees her, so that they thank God and pray for her."

In 1554, Châtelheraut having been persuaded to resign his unsuccessful attempts to govern Scotland, Marie de Guise was named by her daughter official regent: and with another Catholic woman on the English throne — that unhappy Mary Tudor who was to prove one of the disenchantments of history — all seemed to promise well, in spite of the growing virulance of the preacher John Knox. That same year the Queen of Scots was granted her own separate household in France, a dignity which her uncle, the Cardinal, had long been urging. She had now reached the mature age of twelve — older than any of the other royal children — and was entitled to some domestic independence. She had also acquired tastes of her own, and no one seems to have bothered if they were somewhat magnificent ones; except the envious Madame Paroys, who headed her off when she wished to present some of her court dresses to be made into vestments for her aunt's convent. "It gives me a shabby reputation," Mary protested rather tactfully to her mother, "so that people say that I do not resemble you at all." About this time the ubiquitous Cardinal was advising Marie: "In the settlement of your daughter's establishment, it is my opinion that there should be nothing that is either superfluous or mean, for meanness is the thing of all others which she hates most." He was obliged to add that no further help could be expected from the French King, whose finances were at a pretty low ebb and who had already promised to repair various Scotch fortifications.

So a household of just sufficient state, similar to that already granted to the Dauphin, was gathered about Mary: a faithful little group whose chief habitat was in one of the Guise castles at Meudon, but who stood ready to accompany her on her various royal visits. One can imagine the juvenile pride with which she presided at her first official function, a supper for the Cardinal who — as she was to write on that sad later day when news came of his death — had been both uncle and father to her. One can also imagine the cordial but critical eye with which the churchman appraised the results of what he had himself engineered with the thorough-going efficiency of his family. To the young Queen's annoyance, Madame Paroys — who seems to have impressed the Cardinal with her piety and Catherine de Medici with her fidelity — remained in authority as chaperon. But within two years she was replaced by Madame Briante, Mary Seaton's mother, who had settled in France and made a French marriage. And to have the four Marys of her childhood once again as playmates and ladies-in-waiting, with the devoted Janet Sinclair and John Kemp in attendance, brought a homey feeling into the state regulations of her young life.

But now more than ever the Cardinal superintended the studies of his niece, and he seems to have been a bit pitiless in his determination to make a queen and a scholar of one whom Mother Nature so obviously had made for a particularly lovable woman. Or was he merely trying to be protective? Did he already recognize Mary's high sensitivity, her magnetism and incipient sex appeal, and with the ancient wisdom of the Church was he consciously practicing what modern psychologists call sublimation? While he was about it he might well have taught her a more realistic insight into human nature! Reports which have come down to us of recurrent attacks of fever and fainting — which the medical simplicity of the times dismissed as indigestion — indicate that he was pushing Mary's adolescence too fast and too far.

But she was not only intelligent, she was a good student who enjoyed study. She read the Latin classics and writings of the saints, Erasmus, and the long cycles of medieval romance. And in addition to rather prolific letters, her little notebooks preserved in the Bibliothèque Nationale are full of Latin themes and French verse. On one historic occasion, when she was about thirteen, she read aloud to the somewhat awed court assembled at the Louvre an original Latin discourse on the higher education of women! In fact, the girl Mary was in some danger of becoming one of those Learned Ladies who have been so often the subject of Gallic satire.

Lᒐᒐᒐᒐᒐᒐᒐᒐᒐᒐᒐᒐᒐᒐᒐᒐᒐᒐᒐᒐᒐᒐᒐᒐᒐᒐᒐᒐᒐ

CHAPTER IV

THE BRIDE

Mary Stuart was, of course, too lovely to be satirized: she could only, as future years were to show, be slandered or adored. The French court — to a man, and almost to a woman — chose the latter path. Already young Henri de Montmorency was arousing royal jealousy by his obvious but innocent devotion, while his father the Constable did not hesitate to throw out the rather sage suggestion that the danger of Scotch insurrection might be lessened if the young Queen married a French nobleman who could live with her in that troubled country, rather than the future King of France. All this was highly distasteful and politically heretical to both Henri II and the Guises, who — with Calais recovered and peace again between France and England — decided it was time for the royal marriage to take place. Mary was now almost sixteen, François almost fifteen: surely old enough to be pushed into more dominating positions on the international chessboard!

King Henri was in many ways an honest and in some ways a pathetic human being, who had suffered all his life from a politic marriage forced upon him for State reasons. But he seems to have learned neither honesty nor pity in dealing with this precarious problem among the royal children he otherwise really loved. He must have known that his sickly,

adolescent François was unfit for marriage and probably incapable of marriage, yet he never hesitated to sacrifice the
radiant young Mary to political expediency; as, a few months
later, he was to sacrifice his own younger daughter, Madame
Ysabel, sending her off weeping to be the third bride of the
morbid Spanish widower, Phillip II. Even the Cardinal of
Lorraine encouraged his niece's marriage as the obvious
fulfillment of her destiny. How could an event so clearly for
the glory of Scotland, of France — and of the house of Guise
— fail also to be for the glory of God?

So the knell began tolling for the death of Mary's happy
and carefree girlhood when, in the autumn of 1557, King
Henri formally invited the Regent and Estates of Scotland
to send their deputies to France to arrange for their Queen's
marriage and the happy cementing of friendship between
the two countries. A kind of coalition commission, part
Catholic, part Protestant, arrived the following February: the
Archbishop of Glasgow and the Bishop of Orkney (the latter
to die before his return), Lord Fleming and Lord Seton,
the Earls of Roth and Cassillis, Sir John Erskine of Dun, *and*
Mary's natural brother, Lord James Stuart. The last two, at
least, had recently been signers of John Knox's Solemn
League and Covenant to uphold the Protestant Congregation
in Scotland and "forsake and renounce the Congregation of
Satan with all the superstitious abominations and idolatry
thereof": meaning, of course, the Holy Catholic and Apostolic
Church of Rome. But by one more paradox of the paradoxi-
cal age, the apostate Stuart bastard still retained his post —
and his revenues — as Prior of St. Andrews, the richest benefice in Scotland; which, by one of the age-old abuses soon to
be corrected by the Council of Trent, had been permitted
to fall to a layman with sufficient political backing in State
or Church.

Mary, with the trustfulness of one used to love and with

a naïveté hard to associate with the court or with her masterful uncles, greeted the commissioners warmly and seemed to take particular delight in talking with her illegitimate kinsman. It was more than five years since she had seen her mother, and the four Marys of her childhood were only recently back from their convent in Poissy — so perhaps some nostalgic call of the Stuart blood drew her to this strange half brother. Her carefully sheltered upbringing and rather exotic education had left her particularly defenseless before the darker sides of human nature, and she kept a kind of invincible ignorance of jealousy and duplicity — although Heaven knows they were plentiful enough in France and superabundant in Scotland! She had absolutely no intuitive knowledge of men. It took her literally years to realize that Lord James Stuart was not honestly intent upon her welfare — rather, in point of fact, upon stealing her throne for himself: just as, later on, it took her years to realize that her "good sister Elizabeth" would not be "honored" to champion her cause when she fled to England. So Mary was all sunshine during that spring of 1558. From childhood she had thought of François as a younger brother whom she must protect and a future husband whom she must please; they had shared their pets, their games, their little secrets. She had grieved over and then taken for granted his many illnesses, and rejoiced now in his too sudden growth and his real excellence in horsemanship. Although sixteen was a fairly mature age in royal France, she seems to have been quite unawakened passionally. What she felt for her adolescent Dauphin was evidently a gently sentimental attachment rooted in ideas of duty and security, flowering into a gently unselfish devotion as the danger of death edged closer to him. If she was being cheated as a woman the girl Queen was the last to guess it, and no one else seemed to care.

There was much signing of tedious papers before the marriage — most of it rather meaningless to Mary, and scarcely important enough to interfere with the little holiday granted at her favorite château of Chenonceaux. One document was an assurance to the Scottish Parliament that her marriage would not interfere with their national liberties, another had to do with her French dowry, which was to include the duchy of Touraine and the county of Poitou. And upon her return to Fontainebleau in April, she was introduced by the secret diplomacy we have not yet outgrown to another mysterious batch of papers, which today seem either meaningless or malignant. In one of them she announced that in case of her death without issue Henri II was to become King of Scotland — in another she stipulated that, under the same improbable circumstances, her kingdom was to be handed over to him until a large payment in gold was made by the Scotch to defray the expenses of his military aid and her own French residence and education. It all seems rather fatuous to the modern student, since either program would have precipitated war with England or Spain or both. But Mary signed at the request of her future father-in-law and with the sanction of her uncles. All her life she was to share — as Elizabeth Tudor shared also — the curious political tenet of the times that a kingdom belonged to its monarch, and in the absence of a direct heir could be assigned more or less according to that monarch's whim.

So the wedding plans progressed bravely, with the formal betrothal or "handfasting" of bride and groom taking place on April 19th at the Louvre. On the following Sunday morning — April 24th, 1558 — Paris woke to one of the most overwhelming pageants it had yet witnessed, celebrating the first marriage of a dauphin in his home country for two hundred years. The architect Le Conte had built a beautifully arched platform, decorated with pale blue hangings

and golden fleurs-de-lis, which extended from the door of
the archbishop's palace to the main entrance of Notre Dame
Cathedral. Opposite was a large and ornate dais to accommo-
date the chief nobles and Scotch commissioners; while below,
the Place du Parvis was breathlessly crowded with soldiers,
burghers, magistrates upon their mules, students, thieves,
the more adventurous householders and women, who made
up the "infinite variety" of the King's "good city."

At precisely eleven o'clock the shrill trumpets sounded,
and the Archbishop of Paris, Eustache du Bellay, with his
cross-bearer and attendants, opened the great door of his
cathedral — while from the door of his neighboring palace
emerged a company of Swiss guards followed by the redoubt-
able Duc de Guise, idol of France and grand marshal of
the day's ceremonies. Then across the Gothic platform the
procession unfolded: musicians in red and gold, one hundred
gentlemen clothed in the glory of the court, seven cardinals
and some eighteen bishops and abbots in the greater glory
of the Church — the frail Dauphin François, a little wan
in his puffed cloth of gold, escorted by his cousin the King
of Navarre (O politics!) and followed by his far-from-sturdy
little brothers, the future Charles IX and Henri III. There
was more braying of trumpets, more delicate music: then
King Henri II led through the palace doorway the tall and
radiant young bride, crowned with jewels. The nobles and
their wives gasped, for contrary to the gorgeous custom of
the day Mary was wearing her favorite white — the color
associated with royal mourning in France — white damask,
shimmering with encrusted pearls and diamonds, from which
a train of blue velvet was supported by two lucky little
maids of honor. She was followed by Catherine the Queen
Mother and the powerful Protestant Prince de Condé. But
Scotland was so close to civil war that Mary's own mother
had not dared to leave: Marie de Guise's place at the wedding

upon which she had staked so much being taken by her own
mother, the aged Duchess Antoinette.

The marriage ceremony — probably again for State or
political reasons — was preformed not by the Cardinal of
Lorraine but by the Cardinal de Bourbon. At its close and
after a learned allocution by the Archbishop of Paris, the
royal cortege was followed by the noble guests into the
tapestry-draped cathedral, where a nuptial Mass was celebrated at the high altar. Meanwhile, from the gallery outside, such *largesse* was thrown to the people that finally, in
fear of being trampled under one another's feet, they begged
for no more.

A collation for the royal guests was served in the archbishop's palace, after which came music and the stately
dancing of the time. And about midafternoon the cavalcade
— Kings and Princes on horseback, the two Queens in a
litter, beside which walked their Eminences of Lorraine and
Bourbon — set out for the Palais de Justice. Here another
and more elaborate banquet was served, followed by more
dancing, a procession of sportive hobbyhorses and a typically
Renaissance masque of the Seven Planets. It was the wish
both of the King and the scarcely less important House of
Guise that this royal merrymaking should be shared by as
many as possible: not only were the representatives of Scotland honorably seated and the municipal fathers of Paris
given honorable standing room, but the windows were
opened wide so that the populace outside might have a
view — an opportunity which they improved to the extent
of perching upon the statues and climbing upon the balconies
of the Palais de Justice.

One wonders what the inscrutable Lord James Stuart
thought of the final scene of this pageant, when five miniature
ships of gold with silver sails were mysteriously propelled
across the floor. On each deck were two chairs, one already

occupied by a prince of the blood royal, the other awaiting the lady of his choice. By a gracious gesture the Dauphin signaled to his somewhat eclipsed mother, Catherine de Medici; but King Henri lifted the young Mary to his own chair of state, while the ships sailed off to gentle music on their dream voyage. . . .

The girl bride was enchanted but evidently not in the least exalted by this frank adulation. When it was all over she took time out like a good child to write her absent mother in Scotland how grateful she was for the priceless wedding gifts and for the great "honor and friendship" shown by her two uncles in directing the whole celebration. "I will say no more, except that I think myself one of the happiest women in the world," she concluded formally. But she did say more: with eloquent ingenuousness she gave the reasons for her happiness — how she had received from the King and Queen of France all that she could possibly hope, "and from the King my husband an esteem in which I could wish to live and die!"

What more could even a royal bride expect?

CHAPTER V

QUEEN OF FRANCE

M ARY had hoped to pass her honeymoon at
her beloved château of Chenonceaux which, bridging the
river Cher, blends something of the charm of Venice with
the charm of France. But as usual, her preference was overruled — perhaps because at the time Chenonceaux was identified with Diane de Poitiers, and so considered by the Guises
unsuitable for the royal bride. It is more than a little curious
to notice how consistently the wishes of this "absolute" young
Queen were directed or deflected by other people all along.
At any rate, the choice which fell upon Villers-Cotterets, a
spacious and beautiful property of her mother's family in the
country near Soissons, was not an unhappy one. It was
further north and cooler than Chenonceaux, with miles of
forest paths through which Mary and François could ride or
walk; and here the royal "babes in the woods," returning
to their lessons and their music between those outdoor ram-
bles, passed one of the most idyllic interludes of their
troubled lives.

But is *was* an interlude, and soon over. Within a few
months the King, although busy drawing up peace treaties
with both Spain and England, thought fit to order his son
the Dauphin off for military training at the camp near
Amiens. And the end of November brought news more

revolutionary to Europe in general and Mary Stuart in particular than anyone at the time realized. This was the death of Mary Tudor and her succession on the English throne by the twenty-five-year-old Elizabeth. In 1536 Henry VIII had declared this daughter of Anne Boleyn illegitimate and ordered Parliament to bar her from the throne, although a few years before his death he relented sufficiently to name her an unlikely third in line of succession. Now, ironically enough, the high-tempered, bad-mannered, vacillating but vital young woman became Queen of a country whose late Renaissance was just about to round the full circle of its glory. In the eyes of Catholic Europe and of the large remaining section of English Catholics, she was, in Hilaire Belloc's plain words, "certainly illegitimate by all the moral canons of the day."* By these same canons, particularly the old allegiance to the royal blood stream, the next lawful heir to the English throne was Mary of Scotland, granddaughter on her father's side of Henry VIII's sister Margaret, and great-granddaughter of King Henry VII. When it became evident that for political reasons Elizabeth — whose personal religious inclination seems to have been mildly toward the Catholic side — was determined to undo the blundering work of her predecessor and to champion Protestantism, she loomed up as a menace as well as a usurper.

In this political and religious crisis Henri of France — who had taken quite a different attitude where the Scottish throne was in question — immediately took the legitimist side and determined that Mary's claim should be duly registered before Europe. He had no intention of fighting England to uphold it, of course, having neither the will nor the money for any more wars: but he saw to it that his daughter-in-law should make the suitable gesture. So the

----

* *Characters of the Reformation.*

arms of England suddenly appeared upon the young couple's silver and on their heraldic banners — an act which nobody took very seriously, as such quarterings were frequently used by any proximate heir of a royal family. Far more unwisely, and of course quite uselessly, either Henri or the ambitious Guise uncles — or both — insisted upon young Mary signing her official documents "Queen of Scotland, England, and Ireland" as well as "Dauphiness of Guienne." This she did a few times, as an empty form and against her own will, she later explained to Elizabeth. But the latter never forgot. She was too uncertain of the validity of her own claims to afford forgetfulness or forgiveness, either! And when the controversial Treaty of Edinburgh came up for discussion, probably its most controversial clause demanded that Mary and her husband should abstain "in all times coming" from assuming English arms or titles: a demand which even Cecil, Elizabeth's omnipotent Lord Treasurer, admitted to be, under the circumstances, quite impossible to enforce.

But all such small problems and peccadillos were soon pushed aside by the terrific shock of a lance which, at the end of a day's playful jousting, took the King's eyesight and on July 10th his life. Within a few weeks Henri II was laid beside his forefathers in the abbey of St. Denis, while in the cathedral of Rheims François and Mary were consecrated King and Queen of France. She was not quite seventeen, he a year younger; so it seems to have been taken for granted that State decisions should be shouldered by the Guise uncles and domestic ones by Catherine de Medici — an antipathetic partnership certain to bring trouble. Nevertheless, the youngsters were actual sovereigns, and their brief court became one of the most cultured and also one of the most innocent in Europe. Ronsard the "Prince of Poets," du Bellay, and the irrepressible Brantôme were its literary leaders, who vied with one another through prose and verse in perfectly sincere adoration of the tall, pale, but radiant young Queen. *"O belle et plus que belle,"* cried the enchanted (and highly experienced) Pierre de Ronsard, to whom some luminous quality about Mary suggested dawn and the morning star. And years later Brantôme was to recall how "above all, she delighted in poetry and poets," whose work he had seen her read "with tears in her eyes."

Two notes of deepening discord obtruded into this harmony. The first was the ominous growth of the Huguenot movement with its revolutionary political implications, both national and international; for it was already evident that every revolt of French or Scottish Protestants could count upon the covert help of Elizabeth and England. One of the most important of these uprisings came in the March of 1560, led by one Bary de la Renaudie, a French adventurer of not too savory reputation; although it was more than hinted that the real leader was the Prince de Condé, encouraged by Catherine de Medici and Elizabeth — who were at the time on terms of suspicious intimacy. In any case, the object of the plot was to murder the Duc de Guise and his brother the Cardinal, to imprison François and Mary, and to set up a new government by the Huguenots. This was to have come to a head while the court was in peaceful residence at Blois; but when word of the conspiracy filtered through to the vigilant Cardinal of Lorraine, he promptly and quietly removed the royal household to the greater security of the huge château of Amboise. Here the conspirators followed, gathering their forces in the nearby woods and preparing their attack, when they were overtaken and captured by royal troops led by de Guise himself. The Queen Mother and de Condé promptly turned prosecutors or "state's evidence"; and there were mass executions of the traitors, including de la Renaudie — who was hanged upon a scaffold in full view of the château. It was just a particularly horrible example of sixteenth-century revolt and reprisal, and an eloquent sermon upon that fatal mixing up of politics and religion which threatened to disrupt European civilization.

A credible tradition describes how Queen Mary, forced to show herself with her husband on one of the château balconies while the executions were in progress, fell into a faint which left her in a strangely rigid condition. To the modern mind this reaction seems natural enough. It was less natural that others of these too-frequent swoons should have caused her to be carried out of church and away from a State dinner, or that she should have become increasingly subject to sudden gusts of tears. Of course the hopeful court at first attributed such symptoms to a possible pregnancy: before long, it began to suspect a quite opposite cause. For the age itself was highly neurotic — without as yet analyzing the meaning of neuroticism — and an unconsummated marriage was a recognized if secret source of danger. But Mary walked bravely through these months of tension, alone so far as any sympathetic understanding went. For her mother was still in Scotland, fighting with her back to the wall; Diane de Poitiers was living in retirement after Henri's death; while his sister Marguerite (the Duchess of Savoy) and his daughter Ysabel — both her particularly close friends — were removed from the court by their own marriages. There remained her loving but inexperienced group of Marys, her growingly hostile Florentine mother-in-law, the uncles to whom she was always less a woman than a pawn of statecraft, and the failing, faithful boy she loved and called husband. "The Scottish Queen in my opinion looketh very ill," commented Throckmorton, the English ambassador at Paris. And another of Cecil's agents wrote back to his master with mock piety: "God take her to Him as soon as may please Him!"

Meanwhile Marie de Guise was nearing the end of her Scottish Purgatory. From the time she assumed the regency in 1554 matters had grown worse instead of better. She was high-souled and high-hearted, but no match for a nobility thirsting for her power plus a populace increasingly hostile to her religion. Yet every time she turned for protection to the French troops or French advisers she could trust, she seemed to increase the danger of revolt. Even the expenses of their young Queen's marriage were resented by the Scotch parliament; and soon after that event Marie realized — as her daughter, of course, did not — that at least two of the native nobles were actually conspiring to steal her throne. These were the bastard Lord James Stuart in Scotland and the young Earl of Arran, Châtelheraut's eldest son, in France: both of whom were receiving help from Elizabeth. By 1559 anti-Catholic fanaticism had been so successfully energized by John Knox that churches and religious houses all over Scotland were being looted and profaned. From St. Andrews in the north to Stirling and Edinburgh the desecration swept on like a diabolically directed whirlwind; and Knox's own description of how the Reformers forced the monks of Lundores Abbey to stand by while their altars were overthrown, "their idols, vestments of idolatry and mass books burned in their own presence, and they commanded to cast away their monkish habits," is merely a macabre detail of the general picture.

By the autumn of that year Marie de Guise was formally repudiated as Regent by the "Lords of the Congregation" and civil war swept the country in earnest. Before long the youthful Duke of Norfolk arrived with an army sent by Elizabeth to bolster up the Protestants. Marie with her pitifully small French garrison and the Catholic nobles who remained faithful fought on, although Leith was already suffering from famine. She was practically a prisoner in

Edinburgh Castle when, in the June of 1560, Death sent his merciful emissaries, offering the peace she had always desired but had known so little.

"Great responsibilities are easy to assume but difficult to carry well before God," Marie had written wearily a few years before to her brother the Cardinal, adding that "sorrow of the soul surpasseth all other pains." Now, in all humility, she invited the noblemen who had made her life unbearable to come for a final conference, and as they stood beside her bed — the arch-traitors Châtelheraut and Lord James Stuart, with the Counts of Argyle, Glencairn, and others — she begged their loyalty for her daughter the Queen, and advised sending both French and English troops away from Scotland as soon as possible. Then she gave them her pardon and asked theirs, offering to each her cheek or her hand to kiss. It was a very Christian death: although the pervert earls who had refused her prayer for a priest would not permit a Christian or "Popish" funeral. Not until three months later was the leaden coffin containing her body borne back to France and interred in her brother's city of Rheims.

Meanwhile, news of her death had of course reached France, but even the Cardinal feared at first to tell his niece. It was the first major grief to strike the young Mary and she was devastated, passing — in the words of the Venetian ambassador — "from one agony to another." With danger-ously dry eyes she knelt through the great Requiem sung in Notre Dame Cathedral, and heard her mother lauded for her "viril heart in a woman's body." Strangely enough, that mother had reached the very age destiny was reserving for Mary Stuart — forty-five years.

> "When sorrows come, they come not single spies
> But in battalions,"

the Queen's own younger contemporary, Shakespeare, was

to write: and he might well have had Mary herself in mind
when he penned the words. All through the summer and
early autumn of 1560, the health of her boy husband was
obviously weakening; and a fiendish rumor started by the
Huguenots to the effect that François was touched with
leprosy and could only be healed by bathing in the blood of
young children, terrified the peasants and brought one more
grief to the royal pair. In October there was a convocation
of the Estates General at Orléans, and the King and Queen
made a magnificent formal entry, wearing their crowns and
followed by representatives of the clergy, the army, the civil
guilds, and the university students. But just as they were
preparing to leave at the end of November, François contracted a heavy cold which his long invalidism was unable to
fight. An exact diagnosis of this final illness is difficult today,
but reports of an "imposthume" or abscess working from
the brain through the ear suggest a possible mastoiditis. The
surgeon's wish to operate was refused by Catherine de Medici,
from what reasons we are left to guess. But all voices unite
in stories of the young Queen's devoted care, even Throckmorton describing her as weakened by her "long watching"
during his illness and "painful diligence about him."

It was without avail. In the chilly early hours of December
6th — barely six months after her mother's death and two
days before her own eighteenth birthday — Mary Stuart was
left a widow.

CHAPTER VI

THE WIDOW

T HE etiquette of French royal mourning was uncompromising and unmerciful. It decreed that the Queen Dowager should pass forty days of strict confinement in a darkened room, during most of which she was supposed to remain in bed and to receive only the most necessary visitors. Mary, staying on at Orléans, conformed perfectly as she always had: her grief and isolation of heart were extreme, and quiet was what she needed most. It is good to remember the prompt and sincere letter sent by Pope Pius IV, commending the young widow to the "Father of mercies and God of all consolation." About the same time John Calvin was writing to one of his coreligionists: "Did you ever read or hear of anything more timely than the death of the little King? . . . God suddenly revealed Himself from heaven, and He who had pierced the father's eye struck the ear of the son."

To the sympathy expressed by Philip II Mary replied early in 1561, assuring "Monsieur my good Brother" that his words had comforted "the most afflicted poor woman under heaven, God having bereft me of all that I loved and held dear on earth." This was truth, not rhetoric; but in the sorrow and loneliness of those weeks she was finding herself. When she officially emerged in her white mourning — "le deuil blanc" which Janet and Ronsard have immortalized for us — the pretty and precocious child exploited by the Cardinal, the docile, delicate, delectable girl exploited by the court, had become a woman capable of facing if not always of solving the problems of her life. She could no longer lean heavily upon her famous uncles, who — resisting the possible temptation of a Guise *coup* — had temporarily retired into obscurity, leaving the court to Catherine de Medici and her Huguenot advisers, the Constable de Montmorency, the Admiral Coligny, and the pervert Cardinal de Châtillon. Sir James Melville does not hesitate to record that Catherine was "blythe" at the death of her son François, and that Mary Stuart was soon being advised by her friends to return to Scotland "rather than to abide the Queen Mother's disdain in France."

Almost immediately, of course, the question of Mary's remarriage came up — a question in which she seems to have taken small personal interest but in which she was willing to co-operate, knowing a young widowed Queen to be a dangerous anomaly in European politics. Emotionally she appears to have been still quite unawakened; and the one man in France who might have wakened her to happiness — Montmorency's son, the devoted Monsieur d'Anville — was all too safely removed both by his Protestant affiliations and his politic marriage some two years before to the granddaughter of Diane de Poitiers. The traitorous young Earl of Arran (Châtelheraut's son) had already presented himself as suitor, as had the King of Sweden and the King of Denmark. But the most serious and powerful prospects were two adolescents — Mary's brother-in-law, Charles IX, and the fifteen-year-old Don Carlos of Spain: both of whom were promptly blackballed by Queen Catherine, already jealously determined to end Mary's prestige in European politics. Then the Cardinal of Lorraine, returning from one of the sessions of the Council of Trent, offered the interesting suggestion of Archduke Charles of Austria, brother of the Emperor Maximilian, and for awhile negotiations were carried on. It is even recorded that the matchmaking Countess of Lennox dispatched her immature but not unattractive son, Henry Darnley, from London as bearer of cousinly sympathy to the widowed Queen. For the time being he failed to attract any particular attention.

Mary must have found it restful to pass the end of Lent and Easter among so many of her own family at Rheims, although the problems went along with her. Once again she retired for peace to the convent of St. Pierre-les-Dames — and once again she was brought back to her queenly duties by the indomitable Cardinal. He was probably right, by all dictates of worldly wisdom: but one wonders if he had not something to answer for in the tangled and tragic pattern of her later life.

In any case, when Mary Stuart left Rheims in April it was definitely decided that she should return to her own kingdom of Scotland. Brantôme, who was to be among the group accompanying her, assures us that the young Queen would have preferred "a hundred times more to remain in France a simple dowager, and content herself with Touraine and Poitou for her dowry, than to go reign in her savage country: but messieurs her uncles, at least some if not all of them, counselled her to go." So another wish of the woman was frustrated — but the Queen had become determined to play out her assignment with destiny as capably and fearlessly as destiny would permit. Before she reached the Duke of Guise's property at Joinville, where she planned to tarry a few weeks, she was overtaken by a messenger from her Scotch Catholic subjects, Canon John Leslie, the future Bishop of Ross. He brought assurances of the allegiance of Huntley and the Catholic north, advising her to disembark at Aberdeen

and proceed to her stormy capital protected by an army of
some twenty thousand faithful subjects. Mary listened carefully and courteously, although the armed approach was
never to her taste.

Then within a day or two arrived the emissary of the
opposite camp — no other than her natural brother Lord
James Stuart, whose counsel was quite the contrary. It would
seem that Mary and her usually astute uncle the Cardinal
were strangely ignorant of Lord James' activities against
Marie of Guise, of his conspiracies to assume the Scottish
crown with Protestant support, and of the fact that he came
now straight from a London interview with his patron Queen
Elizabeth. For Mary received him with her customary sweet-
ness and confidence, and decided to follow his advice about
sailing direct to Leith and throwing herself upon the promised loyalty of her subjects. He left her early in May, swearing fealty "to the uttermost of his power," and — in the
probably unconscious irony of Melville's words — going
ahead to Scotland "to prepare the hearts of the subjects
against her homecoming." Incidentally, he stopped off *en
route* to report the whole plan to Elizabeth and Cecil, and is
said to have advised the possible intercepting of the Scottish
Queen on the seas.

Mary was in no haste to make the final turning of this
page of her life. She tarried for the baptism of a young Guise
kinsman at Nancy, for a last visit with her grandmother at
Joinville, and with her uncle the Cardinal in the shadow of
his majestic cathedral at Rheims. On June 10th she reached
Paris, where she was royally welcomed — since she was no
longer considered dangerous! — by the young King Charles
IX, the Queen Mother, the King of Navarre, and Prince de
Condé. The English Ambassador Throckmorton was in the
French capital, and illuminating vignettes of Mary are found
in the copious and certainly not overindulgent letters he sent

back home. He details one visit in which he begged her — as he had shortly after King François's death — to ratify that Treaty of Edinburgh which her hostile subjects had drawn up with England shortly after the death of Marie de Guise: one clause of which included her renouncement of all future claims upon the English throne. With her precise but gracious poise and no little diplomacy, Mary refused to sign the document until she should have the opportunity of discussing so important a subject with her own people. When Throckmorton brought the conversation around to the still more controversial subject of religion, she replied with disarming candor: "I will be plain with you, and tell you what I would all the world should think of me. The religion I profess I take to be most acceptable to God; and indeed neither do I know nor desire to know any other. Constancy doth become all folks well, but none better than princes . . . especially in matters of religion." Then the young Queen added that while she had heard many disputations and found no reason to change her own opinions, she had no desire to "constrain" her subjects in this matter.

No wonder the ambassador reported somewhat ruefully that Mary showed herself "of great wisdom for her years and of equal modesty, and also of great judgment in the handling of herself and her matters. . . . She carries herself so honourably, advisedly and discreetly that one cannot but fear her progress." There were special reasons for this last reference to Mary's spotless personal behavior through all this difficult time. For over a year Elizabeth's liaison with Dudley, the future Earl of Leicester — whose wife Amy Robsart had recently died under suspicious circumstances — had become a scandal throughout Europe and the gossip of Madrid and Paris as well as London. "One laugheth at us, another threateneth, another revileth the Queen," Throckmorton wrote privately to the Marquis of Northampton; adding with mortification, "All the estimation the English had got is clear gone."

Meanwhile the Queen of Scots prepared for her departure, making an inventory of her wardrobe and jewels and arranging the thousand details of her journey. Having been advised that English ships were patrolling the coast and that her royal cousin's attitude toward her return was none too friendly, she dispatched M. d'Oysel to London to obtain formal assurance from Elizabeth of her safe passage through English waters. Doubtless to his humiliation, Throckmorton had to report that his royal mistress not only refused this courtesy but had flown into a violent temper before the court while discussing it. Mary listened with dignity, protesting still her wish to be friends with her sister monarch. But there must have been fire in her Stuart eyes when she announced that she would return to her own realm with or without Elizabeth's permission. "I trust the wind will be so favorable as I shall not need to come on the coast of England; and if I do, then, Monsieur l'Ambassadeur, the Queen your mistress shall have me in her hands to do her will of me." Mary ended the interview on a note of curious and dreamy prophecy: "If she be so hard-hearted as to desire my end she may then do her pleasure. Peradventure that casualty might be better for me than to live!"

On Friday, August 14th — thirteen years almost to the day since her happy arrival on the Breton coast — the Scottish Queen embarked upon one of the two galleys waiting at Calais. The great Guise uncles, who had welcomed and watched her so hopefully, must have had both head and heart heavy with misgiving as they bade her farewell. Their three younger brothers — the Duc d'Aumale, the Grand Prior of France, and the roistering Marquis d'Elboeuf — who were accompanying her to Scotland, probably thought of little beyond the adventure and the pleasant companionship of the four Marys. It was a strangely assorted entourage on ship-board: including three friends Mary was to find faithful unto death — the chatty Brantôme, Leslie, the future Scotch bishop, and de la Mauvissière, the future French ambassador; and at least two — her former Latin professor, Buchanan, and the foolish French poet, Châtelard — who were to lend a hand in her downfall. Almost certainly, too, among the Scotch emissaries upon the galley was James Hepburn, the redheaded, swashbuckling Earl of Bothwell, hereditary Grand Admiral of Scotland, and like his father the Earl Patrick, always a loyal supporter of Marie de Guise. At this time he was about twenty-five years old and had already earned some reputation as a reckless leader of men and an unscrupulous seducer of women. He professed Protestantism, but his re-ligion seems to have been little more than a violent and blustering antipathy to the Old Faith. With all this, he was the best Border captain Scotland could boast and, although perpetually short of money, one of the few lords incorruptible by English bribes. It might have been enlightening if Mary had taken this time to study the perverse champion upon whom her future was so perversely to hang. Perhaps she had already heard his sneering calumny that the Queen of England and the Queen of Scotland together would not make one honest woman. Or perhaps she was merely too unhappy to be interested in men at all.

Her heart and eyes, too, were full of tears as the galleys drew out of the harbor. She refused to leave her place in the stern for supper, and even had her couch made up there for the first night of the journey, so she might see the gray, receding coast line of the land she loved until the last pos-sible moment. *"Adieu, France, c'en est fait,"* she kept mur-muring between her sobs: *"Adieu, France — je pense ne vous revoir jamais plus!"*

No doubt the sympathetic Brantôme and the Marys and

the young Guise uncles tried to reassure her with promises
of an early return visit to the country of which she remained
Dowager Queen. But her intuition was tragically correct.
C'en est fait — it was indeed over: never would she look upon
France again. . . . She was indifferent to the cold dense fog
in which the vessel was soon enveloped; a fog in which the
ship bearing her horses and some of her furnishings was taken
captive upon the English coast, but thanks to which her own
escaped both North Sea pirates and the stealthy hunters of
Elizabeth. Characteristically, only one impulse was strong
enough to break through her stupor of misery: this was when
she gave her pitiful order that no lash was to be laid upon
the galley slaves to hasten the voyage.

CHAPTER VII

THE HOMECOMING

PROBABLY every biography of Mary Stuart ever written mentions the ominous and impenetrable fog or haar through which, by almost a miracle of seamanship, her galley slipped into the harbor of Leith early in the morning of August 19th. No preparations had been made to welcome her: which must have seemed mysterious to those ignorant of Lord James's hopeful little conspiracy with Elizabeth and the admitted fact of English vessels patrolling the entire coast. So the returning Queen was given temporary shelter in the house of one Captain Lamb, while horsemen were dispatched to Edinburgh with news of her arrival.

It was not long before her mortified and mystified bastard brother rode up — also the old Duke of Châtelheraut and his psychopathic son, the Earl of Arran, still smarting under the dual humiliation of his refusal by both Mary and Elizabeth. In this dubious company, and shabbily mounted upon horses assembled there at Leith, the royal party set out late in the afternoon for the capital. It was a dour and dismal journey for a Queen's homecoming: as different as well could be from the triumphal march which had welcomed the child to France back in the summer of 1548. Obviously Lord James had sent no sufficient notice to Huntley and the other Catholic nobles. And if Mary noticed the meeting between the Earl of Arran

and the Earl of Bothwell — a cold spark of the old feud of
the Hamiltons and the Hepburns — she may have begun to
suspect what it would mean to live among these hostile feudal
barons, far more intent upon their own dignity than the
dignity of their sovereign.

But there were no tears in her eyes as she mounted her
horse and cantered through the Scotch countryside wrapped
in its mist of purple heather. Few incidents obtruded upon
the trip, but such as came were significant. Once the cortege
was interrupted by a band of poor village clerks, who had
just rescued a group of their companions from the prison
where they had been shut up by the Covenanters for per-
forming a Robin Hood masque on Sunday. Their ringleader
had actually been sentenced to death; so hearing that the
Queen was passing by, the young men came begging for
justice and mercy. Of course she promptly acquiesced — and
the whole group promptly and happily joined the procession
to Edinburgh.

A few bonfires had been lighted on the hills outside the
city, and the streets were crowded with curious citizens come
out to watch the royal arrival, but Holyrood House was in
shabby shape to receive the Queen and her companions.
While Mary was preparing for bed that night a rather dread-
ful din rose from the courtyard, where a large group of her
Scotch subjects were shouting psalms to the accompaniment
of off-key rebecs and fiddles. The disgusted Brantôme later
described it as a particularly "vile" performance: but Mary
sweetly sent down a messenger to thank them for their
welcome and to hope they would return to serenade her some
other evening.

The next day she began her long and tortuous task of
rediscovering Scotland. She can scarcely have remembered
Edinburgh, since so little of her childhood had been spent
in the stormy capital. Now she and her Marys and the French

followers investigated Holyrood House, that spacious and really beautiful palace built around its square courtyard by her grandfather, James IV. Close beside it was the battered twelfth-century Norman abbey which the canons of St. Augustine had long served — first as a shrine for that relic of the True Cross which the English later stole away from them. For the next six years this "house" was to be Mary's chief home, and probably her feminine taste was already planning to increase its comfort by the furnishings she had brought from France. She could look out from its upper windows upon High Street, at whose far end rose the ancient castle or citadel high upon the rock which even Ptolemy had mentioned. Originally it had been a Pictish stronghold, and it was believed to be the Castle of Maidens referred to in Arthurian romance. Mary, gazing up at the mysterious pile, knew that it contained the primitive chapel of Malcolm's Queen, St. Margaret — and the room where her own mother, Marie de Guise, had died. What she could not know was that she herself was to be driven within its stone walls for safety's sake before the birth of her only son.

But people are more important than places: and under the guidance of her cryptic brother Lord James, Mary began making weighty new acquaintances. One of the most weighty was William Maitland, the Laird of Lethington — a Protestant himself, but son of one of her mother's loyal protectors. He was a learned man, a subtle courtier, and a highly efficient politician, already on terms of questionable intimacy with England. It was he who had tried unsuccessfully to arrange the marriage between Arran and Elizabeth; and he more than any other had engineered that pro-English Treaty of Edinburgh which Mary had wisely refused to ratify. Now he was all conciliation — in fact, he seems to have been coerced almost against his will into admiration for the young Queen. She, as usual, promptly forgave and forgot: and, no doubt influenced by her brother's reports, put more confidence in Lethington than in the blunt and burly leader of the Gordon Highlanders, George, Earl of Huntley, who soon presented himself as ambassador from the Catholic Highlands. Another to whom she gave her quick and fatal trust was James Douglas, Earl of Morton, son of the Douglas clan which had been hereditary Stuart enemies.

On the first Sunday after her arrival Mary naturally planned to have Mass offered in her chapel at Holyrood, by the chaplain — René Benoit — who had accompanied her from France. She was utterly unprepared for the storm of hostile fury this announcement let loose. How could she know that the preacher John Knox — who, during the interregnum following her mother's death, had become both religious and political tyrant of Edinburgh — was proclaiming he would rather ten thousand French soldiers should march into the capital than that one Mass should be celebrated there? So on the morning of August 24th, when the priest and his acolyte were peacefully crossing the courtyard, they were violently set upon by various Lords of the Congregation (as the Protestants styled themselves) while threats were heard that "the idolater priest shall die the death." Only the protection of Lord James Stuart — already chafing under the Knox brand of fanaticism — who stood sword in hand at the chapel door, permitted the Queen and her entourage to complete their distracted devotions.

The next morning a royal proclamation was attached to the Market Cross of Edinburgh, announcing with rare patience that the Queen's Majesty "understood the great inconvenience that may come through the division presently standing in the Realm for the difference in matters of Religion," and was most desirous of seeing it pacified "to the honour of God and tranquillity of her Realm": for which purpose she had taken the godly resolution to call a general meeting of her Estates (the Scottish Parliament) that by their advice some solution might be found "to the contentment of the whole." In the meantime both sides were ordered to "keep peace and civil society among themselves"; and anyone who should attempt to overthrow the form of religion which her Majesty found publicly standing upon her arrival was to be considered a "seditious person and raiser of tumult," liable to sentence of death. But *also,* by the advice of the Lords of her Secret Council, her Majesty commanded and charged her lieges under the same penalty that none should "molest or trouble" any of her own servants or persons "come out of France in her company." One seems to recognize the suave Maitland in the wording of this manifesto, but the meaning was undoubtedly Mary Stuart's own. She was issuing that amazing thing, an edict of religious toleration for both sides of the controversy! And very much hers was the gentle peroration, declaring that her Majesty was persuaded "her good and loving subjects" would obey these commands "for the reverence they bear to her person and authority," even if no such proclamation had been issued.

Poor hopeful Mary — if she was a full century ahead of her age in tolerance, she anticipated by some three centuries the modern psychology of optimism! And in spite of protests by a few bigots like the half-mad Arran, her personal charm and almost pathetic simplicity bore quick fruit in winning the support of both the Catholic and Protestant lords who continued to pour into Edinburgh. This tall, pale young Queen still in the black and white of her widowhood — so eager to pardon and even to please — was not in the least like the emissary of Satan John Knox had warned his followers against; and he was not long in perceiving that the "holy water of the court" was cooling their ardor. "I have been here now five days, and at first I heard every man say 'Let us hang the priest,' " a certain Covenanter confided to Lord

Ochiltree; "but after that they have been twice or thrice in the Abbey, all their fervancy was past. I think there be some enchantment whereby men are bewitched!"

There was no doubt that Mary was starting on her difficult road with amazing grace and tact. When she made her delayed state entry into Edinburgh she rode smilingly upon her white charger, with Lord James on one side and on the other the Earl of Huntley. The former, as one of the chief Lords of the Congregation, reassured the Protestants. And Huntley, together with her faithful Captain of the Guards, Arthur Erskine, were vigilant in protecting her Catholic sensibilities by heading off some of the more insulting episodes of the pageants prepared by way of welcome: for instance, the scene in which some of her citizens had fancied it amusing to burn in effigy a priest about to celebrate Mass!

A few days later, when the Queen appointed her Privy Council — again, of course, by the advice of her enigmatic brother — its preponderance of Protestants was both disarming and dangerous. The names included Lord James Stuart and Maitland, Huntley and Châtelheraut, Morton, Bothwell, Erskine, and the Lords of Atholl, Glencairn, Marischal and Argyle. Of these eleven it was decreed that a majority of six should always be at hand to advise her on important State business. But like most committees it soon simmered down to the two most active members. These, unluckily, were Lord James Stuart — upon whom she was soon to bestow his coveted title to the Earldom of Moray — and Maitland of Lethington, whom she soon created Secretary of State. Sir James Melville, Scottish ambassador at large, reports in his *Memoirs* this concentration of power with obvious satisfaction. For Lord James, he assures us, had "great credit with my Lord Robert Dudley" (Elizabeth's Earl of Leicester), while Lethington had "great credit with Cecil" himself. Had Mary so far forgotten the counsels of her uncles, the Duke and the Cardinal, that she asked no questions about this mysterious "credit" at the English court? Or was she, by some subconscious process, identifying her half brother and Maitland with the man of war and the man of intellect upon whom she had been taught to depend through all her happy girlhood in France?

Lꓶꓶꓶꓶꓶꓶꓶꓶꓶꓶꓶꓶꓶꓶꓶꓶꓶꓶꓶꓶꓶꓶ

CHAPTER VIII

THE ENIGMA OF JOHN KNOX

WITH all her dubious choice of advisers, Mary was making progress in Scotland. But she soon learned that the most powerful man in her kingdom, the preacher John Knox, still held aloof in active hostility. His character is an interesting if rather terrible study. It is curious that in spite of Knox's copious correspondence and highly circumstantial *History of the Reformation,* he seems to have been careful to hand on few details about his birth and early life. He was born somewhere between 1505 and 1515; and evidently of peasant stock, for he speaks of himself as "a man of base estate and condition," and acknowledges that for generations his people have owed a feudal allegiance to the Earls of Bothwell. It is possible that he studied at St. Andrews in preparation for the priesthood, for he had a perverse familiarity with both the Scriptures and Catholic theology: although no record of his ordination or even taking a degree has been found. There is a Scottish tradition that he was for awhile connected with the Franciscan Order, which may be corroborated by his pleasant admission that he had been "one of Baal's shaven sort." If there had been any affiliation with St. Francis' sons, some atomic upheaval of head or heart must have taken place in the man to produce his later insane hostility, not to the ecclesiastical abuses of the time

— which would have been sane enough and understandable enough — but to the very fundamentals of the Church, especially the Sacrifice of the Mass. In the absence of direct proof, one concludes that he was at least in minor orders; but when he actually emerges upon the recorded scene — about 1546 — he was known as a notary and a Protestant; a friend of the heretic preacher Wishart and a tutor in various families of the Reformers. After Cardinal Beaton's murder, John Knox moved into St. Andrews Castle as a kind of self-appointed chaplain to the rebels, and with them he was taken prisoner by the French and sent for a time to the galleys. But he was soon pardoned by Henri II; after which he preached for awhile in England and was married to one Margaret or Marjorie Bowes, a bit of an heiress. He thought best to get out of the country when the Catholic Mary Tudor became Queen, but instead of returning to Scotland he drifted to Frankfort in Germany and then to Geneva. Here he doubtless met and consulted with John Calvin: learning more precise Protestant dialectics, but proving too personally pugnacious for Calvin's approval.

For awhile Knox lived peacefully enough with his wife and children at Dieppe, merely scattering heresy around the neighboring French countryside. But neither peace nor obscurity was ever to his taste; so in 1555 he came back to Scotland and proceeded to make the life of the Regent, Marie de Guise, increasingly miserable. By 1557 he had become the acknowledged champion of the Lords of the Congregation, and was chiefly responsible for inciting the peasants of Perth and St. Andrews to their infamous desecration of near-by churches and monasteries. Knox could preach with the fear-some eloquence of a Hebrew prophet or a reforming saint — or, for that matter, of Chaucer's wily Pardoner! — and his pride grew with his reputation. His vitriolic work, *The First Blast of the Trumpet against the Monstrous Regiment of*

Women — an attack upon women rulers in general and Mary Tudor and Marie de Guise in particular — was published in 1558, not unnaturally adding to the civil strife in both their countries. Marie bore with him until the next year, when he was "put to the horn" and declared an outlaw: but apparently Scotch outlaws always came back in short order.

The death of Marie de Guise in 1560 ushered in John Knox's year of triumph, and when the Scottish lords threw off Catholicism as a national religion he was deputed to draw up the Confession of Faith for the new Protestant Kirk. It outdid Calvin in its fanaticism and certainly in its violence. For not only did it proscribe all Papal authority in Scotland, put in claims for the old Church lands, whether held by clergy or nobility, and recommend schools where youth should be trained in the new religion. It also decreed imprisonment and actually death for all who celebrated or even *attended* Mass a third time. In point of fact, John Knox advised the prompt murder of all Catholics, with the confiscation of their goods — anticipating a reversed Massacre of St. Bartholomew, as Andrew Lang points out, some twelve years before the event.

The preacher was indeed going about like a lion, seeking whom he might devour, when in the midst of his progress the lion lost his mate. It is impossible now to fathom this strangely twisted nature — to know whether any humble, human tenderness underlay the fanatical bitterness of the heresiarch and so was capable of hurt. There is a certain crude eloquence in the brief contemporary item that he "was in no small heaviness by reason of the late death of his dear bed-fellow, Marjorie Bowes." It would not be very long before he replaced her by a young girl of sixteen: meanwhile the zeal of his public ministry was unabated. Both the lords and people of "the Congregation" accepted this wholesale anti-Catholicism for awhile, although the nobility soon began to realize that their Protestant Pope was more exigent and far more ubiquitous than the remote and rather easily conciliated Bishop of Rome. But as yet there was no revolt. Knox was supreme in the authority he loved; the Catholic Church seemed banished from the land, while the secular power of Marie de Guise was safely divided among a pack of robber barons whose mutual jealousies could be trusted to hold one another in check.

And then the young Queen Mary returned to Scotland — and Knox, commenting upon the fog which enveloped her homecoming, declared that it typified what "sorrow, dolour, darkness and all impiety" she brought along with her. In point of fact Mary did symbolize about everything Knox detested and feared: for who ever detests without first fearing? She was a woman ruler, against whose "monstrous" authority he had long inveighed. She was a follower and supporter of the Romish religion whose destruction was both his life work and his living. To these orthodox heresies she added the unheard-of novelty of tolerance — which would destroy his power as surely as Rome herself — and had been heard to assert that it was "a sore thing to constrain the conscience." One other danger he quickly sensed in the Queen: she was young and beautiful and physically as well as mentally magnetic. And John Knox — who must almost certainly have taken a vow of chastity early in his life — was quite as uxorious as the Old Testament worthies he was fond of quoting. There can be no doubt that in his disturbed and disturbing make-up some sex complex played as powerful a part as the more generally recognized Messianic complex. It is illuminating to study the historic portrait which has come down, and which — not being royal — was far more exact than official: for it reveals the eyes of a fanatic and the mouth of a sensualist. This was the man who, ten years later when Mary herself was languishing in an English prison, said before his death: "As the world is weary of me, so am I of it!"

But he was far from weary when he stalked into Holyrood House that September day of 1561, in company with Lord James Stuart. He came at the invitation, or rather the command, of the Queen whom he now met for the first time and he came wrapped in his usual garment of self-righteousness. They were a curiously, even symbolically antithetic pair: Knox middle aged and heavily built, with black robe and patriarchal beard, arrogantly waiting to assert his new doctrines; Mary slender and girlish in her mourning, but for once more regal than gracious as she leaned upon the old Faith and old civilization which had produced her — probably annoying the self-conscious preacher by her Stuart habit of looking from the side of her eyes. There was nothing sidelong, however, in the directness with which she saluted "Master John Knox," immediately complaining that he had written a treasonable book against feminine rulers and seemed likely to stir up trouble in Scotland as he had already done in the country of her "sister Elizabeth." This mistaken emphasis proves that Mary had carefully been kept in ignorance of the real situation in her own kingdom, and the activities of John Knox during and after her mother's lifetime. He was quick to take advantage of the slip, pointing out that no charges of violence had been brought against him during his English stay. As for the book, of which he was obviously proud, he implied that while its arguments had never been disproved, they were aimed chiefly at "that Jezebel of England" (the unhappy Mary Tudor), rather than against herself or Elizabeth. But, he added, if the Scottish people were willing to accept a woman, he himself would be as content to live under her Grace "as Paul was to live under Nero," provided her hands were not defiled with the "blood of the saints."

Had the Queen been given to satire she might well have inquired who were "the saints," pointing out that so far the bloodshedding had been on their side, not hers. Instead, she kept her temper — and also kept to her point. Did Master Knox believe it lawful for subjects to oppose their rulers by force?

It was a dangerous question to answer in the sixteenth century, but no one can accuse Knox of cowardice. Also, he knew that the growing idea of the "divine right of kings" commanded small following in Scotland, where his position was probably far more secure than Mary's own. So he replied boldly enough that "If their princes exceed their bounds, and do against that wherefore they should be obeyed, it is no doubt but that they may be resisted, even by power." He went on mumbling something about the people taking the sword from princes and binding their hands if the latter were carried away by "blind zeal" or mad frenzy.

Mary knew where he was leading — to a theocracy with himself as head — and she spoke up deliberately: "I perceive that my subjects shall obey you and not me; and shall do as they list and not what I command. So must I be subject to them and not they to me."

The preacher was taken aback by the boldness of her logic, disclaiming any wish to command and adding emotional words about queens being nurses to their people and a general "subjection unto God and His troubled Church."

Again Mary's candor tore aside the mask of his obliquity. "Yes," she replied calmly, "but you are not the Church that I will nurse. I will defend the Church of Rome, for I think it is the true Church of God."

She had turned the key of his mania and in a moment the man was beside himself. "Your will, Madame, is no reason," he fulminated, "neither does your thought make that Roman harlot to be the true and immaculate spouse

of Jesus Christ." . . . A torrent of blasphemous poison poured
from the lips of Knox, informing his Queen that her Church
was "polluted with all kinds of spiritual fornication, as well
in doctrine as in manners," and that for over five hundred
years it had been "farther degenerated" than the Church of
the Jews which had crucified Christ. For good measure he
added that the Mass was nothing but the "invention of man,"
nowhere mentioned in the Scriptures and an "abomination
before God."

Mary — unlike her cousin Elizabeth! — was always silent
when deeply shocked. When she finally answered, it was with
the most astonishing and mature self-control. "My conscience
does not say so," she replied; and having no wish to argue
further with a fanatic, she threw out a hint of having true
churchmen explain Catholic teachings to Master Knox. Then
she rose from the chair of state and prepared to leave the
room.

Knox — from whose own account this colloquy is handed
down — seems to have perceived that his invitation for the
Queen to come hear *his* teaching at St. Giles was not likely
to be accepted; and as she walked toward the door he called
out an excited wish that she might be "as blessed within the
Commonwealth of Scotland, if it be the pleasure of God, as
ever Deborah was in the Commonwealth of Israel."

So ended the first of many fruitless interviews — in at least
one of which the preacher's abuse reduced his Queen to
tears, by which event he seems to have been slightly shamed.
But his egotism was infuriated by her toleration and indifference, and to one of his followers he confided his conviction: "If there be not in her a proud mind, a crafty wit
and an indurate heart against God and His Truth, my
judgment faileth me." It is interesting to note that about the
same time the very Protestant Maitland of Lethington reported to Cecil in England: "The Queen my mistress be-

haves herself so gently in every behalf as reasonably we can require; if anything be amiss the fault is rather in ourselves. You know the vehemence of Mr. Knox's spirit, which cannot be bridled and doth sometimes utter such sentences as cannot easily be digested by a weak stomach. . . . Surely in her comporting with him, she doth declare a wisdom far exceeding her age." After all, Mary was not quite twenty!

It is impossible not to suspect Knox's hand in the preposterous proclamation soon issued by Archibald Douglas, the Covenanting Provost of Edinburgh. This announced that whereas "certain priests, monks, friars and others of the wicked rabble of the Antichrist the Pope" had recently dared to enter the city in spite of a ruling forbidding their presence, therefore the Provost, Bailiffs, and Deacons ordered this proclamation proclaimed anew, "charging all monks, friars, priests, nuns, adulterers, fornicators and all such filthy persons to remove themselves from this town and boundaries thereof within XXIV hours, under the pain of carting through the town, burning on the cheek, and banishing of the same forever."

Stung by this gratuitous insult to her religion, and doubtless on the advice of Lord James and Maitland, Mary acted quickly. She had the proclamation torn down and immediately removed Douglas and his associates, appointing a new city council in their place. Whereupon the Knox group gave another evidence of their bad faith by forwarding information to the English court only that their new Queen had rescinded the order forbidding "adulterers and fornicators" to enter the pious capital — which, incidentally, seems to have had its share of them already.

Mary had known personal jealousy and official conspiracies in France. This was her first experience of the persistent hate, hypocrisy, and treason which were to prove her eventual undoing.

CHAPTER IX

QUEEN OF SCOTS

I T WOULD be absurd, of course, to imply that Mary Stuart had as yet, or perhaps ever, any full realization of the tumultuous waters through which she would be forced to swim. Nobody has such foreknowledge, which is a good thing, as few would have the temerity to go on swimming — unless, by some merciful miracle, along with the perils were revealed also the beauty of the far harbor: that fifth act of our drama which takes place in Eternity.

But two objectives she did perceive and set out to accomplish. She knew that to be truly Queen of Scotland she must understand her country, so radically different from the France where she had grown up; and she realized increasingly that she must co-operate in all possible ways with her powerful sister Queen across the Border. For this latter purpose Mary dispatched Secretary Lethington to England to "grope" Elizabeth's mind — as if anyone could grope anything so unstable! — and to arrange a meeting where the two cousins could personally discuss their differences. Maitland's first visit was not too satisfactory, in spite of the fact that he was suspiciously *persona grata* at the English court. The Tudor Queen still harped, but more temperately, upon the Treaty of Edinburgh; and she was almost hysterically unwilling to debate the matter of the royal succession. But she did not shut the door upon the discussions. So Mary decided to persevere: in fact, through most of her future life, while free in Scotland or imprisoned in England, she was to be pathetically seeking that interview which Elizabeth so persistently deferred or refused. Meanwhile part of the Scottish Queen's policy was, naturally enough, to keep on friendly terms with Elizabeth's ambassador, Master Thomas Randolph. And the latter asked nothing better than to be in constant attendance upon the royal lady he admired and was charged to spy upon.

Her other goal, to comprehend and conciliate her own difficult people, was the fundamental need. And nothing could be more illuminating than to trace the young Queen's failures and successes during that first year of her Scottish residence. A preliminary step was to see this varied country and its inhabitants at first hand. So before September was out Mary and her chosen cavalcade — the Protestant Lord James, the Catholic Earl of Huntley, her faithful captain Arthur Erskine, her four fond Marys, and a few of the French visitors — set out from Holyrood House on horses bought for the occasion, preceded by three trumpeters, who apparently took the place of the modern drum major. They spent the first night at Linlithgow Castle, where the Queen herself had come into a troubled world, and where Lord James was to meet the assassin's hand a few years hence. Stirling was next in line; and it seemed suitable to Mary that a High Mass should be offered in the chapel which had seen her coronation. Unhappily the angry bigots again broke in: there was rioting among the Covenanters and bloodletting among the churchmen; and this time Lord James was apparently among those who tolerated the outrage which Randolph wryly described as "sport alone for some that were there to behold it." That the iron was gradually entering Mary's soul as she learned at last what the Reformers had done to Scotland was

proved after her visit to Perth and St. Andrews, where she
looked upon the wanton ruin of churches and abbeys, the
lonely altars and crumbling statues — and perceived the same
spirit of destructive fanaticism still at work in the insulting
pageants her subjects insisted upon staging for her delecta-
tion. On one occasion the old, dubious illness came upon her,
so that she fell senseless from her horse and was carried to a
near-by shelter. Randolph — who was an observant fellow,
or he would never have been chosen by Cecil for his post
— was to report before long that the Queen was "always ill
and troubled after any great unkindness or grief of mind."
What neither he nor anyone else apparently realized was that
with a few more psychic blows the loveliest woman in Europe
— the "finest shee that ever was," in the Englishman's own
reluctant words — would fall victim to that shadow of catalepsy or converted hysteria which haunted her until the
bloody final hour when her triumphant spirit rose and con-
quered it.

Mary was soon able to continue her all-too-enlightening
trip, however. Before leaving St. Andrews she was witness
to a bitter quarrel between her bastard brother and her
Chancellor, the Earl of Huntley. What immediately started,
the dispute was the latter's faithful boast that, at the Queen's
word, he could have Mass restored not only in Edinburgh
but in three northern shires. But the true cause was Lord
James's jealousy. Even before his royal sister left France he
had put in a plea for the earldom of Moray (or Murray), a
title not infrequently held by lords of the bar sinister in
Scotland but at present possessed by Huntley. Mary refused
then, and later conferred on her brother temporarily the
earldom of Mar instead. But his ambition was insatiate and
insistent. Although from childhood enjoying the great benefice of St. Andrews, he was determined that the rich holdings
of Moray should belong to him, a left-handed Stuart, and

not to the head of the Gordons: and he had probably decided already that if Huntley's death was the only way to his goal, that was the way he would take. For the time being, however, the quarrel was smoothed over, and the whole party had a fairly peaceful respite at Falkland near Loch Lomond, where Mary's father had died in lonely delirium so soon after hearing of her birth. Then they all rode back rather solemnly to Edinburgh.

The autumn was filled with various more or less significant activities. After the departure of her French guests and relatives — except the roistering young Marquis d'Elboeuf, Mary's young French uncle, who could well have been spared — Mary settled down to a hopeful regime as Queen of Scots. She was eager to correct the abuses she had observed or had been brought to her ears; and having disposed of some needed matters of public drainage and sanitation, she turned her attention to the perennial "law's delays," ordering the Lords of the Sessions to sit "both forenoon and afternoon, three days a week," especially for the relief of poor litigants. And as there was a revival of the more or less continuous Border fighting, she dispatched the Earl of Bothwell to assist Lord James in quelling it. For once they seem to have been willing to act in harmony, although — in spite of their common allegiance to the Protestant cause — they never had much use for each other.

On All Saints' Day the royal chapel was again attacked, and there was actually talk among the more bigoted preachers and people of "taking away the Queen's Mass" entirely. But when the General Assembly of the Reformed Church met in December a growing cleavage between ministers and Lords of the Congregation was apparent; and the Mass question seems to have been temporarily pushed aside by the eagerness of the reformed clergy for financial support. Thanks largely to Maitland, Knox's *Book of Discipline* was not confirmed: and the thrifty Scotch nobility insisted upon keeping two thirds of the old Church revenues, with the remaining third to be divided between the Queen and the Covenanting preachers!

With the cold of winter there was some attempt to bring warmth into life at Holyrood House, with the music and dancing and chess playing and card playing of which Mary had always been fond. And December brought two events with a significance undreamed of at the time. One was the visit of the Sieur de Moretta, ambassador from the Savoy court, who probably wished to discuss a suit for the Queen's hand by Alfonso, Duke of Ferrara. With him came one of those poor but gifted Italian adventurers to be found in every court of Europe at that time — one David Riccio or Rizzio, a slightly deformed musician, the son of a good Piedmontese family, who, while still under thirty years, was said to look already "old and discreet." He had taught music in Italy and possessed an unusually fine bass voice, of which the choir of the royal chapel happened to be badly in need. So it came about that Mary requested his transfer to her own service, and Rizzio remained in Scotland: assisting at Church functions, at masques and other social and secretarial duties, inconspicuously but efficiently for the next few years. "Seigneur Davie," as he was known about the court, shared both the culture and the faith of the transplanted young Queen — but for awhile he seems to have roused no particular Scottish jealousy.

The other episode was less savory, growing out of the forcible attack by Bothwell and the Marquis d'Elboeuf upon a light-minded young woman reported to be the mistress of the Earl of Arran. It was all part of a drunken brawl, but as happened so easily in the Scotland of the time, soon developed into a political fracas, with the town bell ringing an alarm and the armed followers of the Hamiltons (Arran's) and the Hepburns (Bothwell's) having to be kept from one another's throats by Lord James and Huntley. Nothing much came of it all, except that Bothwell was ordered to stay out of town until January 8th "for avoiding of cumber," and d'Elboeuf became more unpopular than ever.

At the beginning of 1562, Edinburgh heard much talk of marrying and giving in marriage. The immediate excitement was Lord James' approaching wedding to the Earl Marischal's daughter, Agnes Keith; and although the Queen did not attend the ceremony in St. Giles Church and hear John Knox warn the couple that if they showed any future lack of zeal for "the Church of God" the bride would be blamed, she entertained the pair with a magnificent banquet at Holyrood House and took part in the usual three-day festivities following. Undoubtedly the question of her own remarriage was much in everyone's mind. Personally, she still inclined toward a Spanish alliance with young Don Carlos, although this was practically ruled out by the opposition of both Catherine de Medici and Elizabeth. The latter was equally antagonistic for political reasons to the suit of the Protestant Eric XIV of Sweden, which was being urged rather strenuously in Scotland. And the old Duke of Châtelheraut, who had never given up hope of seeing Mary united to his wretched son, Arran, sounded out Randolph on the English Queen's probable reactions to that improbable event. The ambassador's report to his superiors was definite enough to be prophetic: "The father," he declared, "is so inconstant, saving in covetousness and greediness, that in three moments he will take five purposes — his son so drowned in dreams men fear that he will fall into some dangerous and incurable sickness, or play one day some mad part that will bring himself to mischief."

Meanwhile the Queen of Scots was still writing trustfully and hopefully to Elizabeth, suing for a private interview to resolve whatever prevented "the quietness of us both" — also for a public, open conclave where commissioners from both countries might discuss and amend the problematical Treaty of Edinburgh. "So far as concerns us," Mary wrote, "we will do all that in reason may be required, or rather enter into a new one, such as may stand without our prejudice, in favor of you and the lawful issue of your body: provided that our interest to that crown, failing yourself and the said issue, may be put in good security." It is unlikely that she suspected at this time what Elizabeth must have known and was trying to conceal from the rest of Europe — that physical abnormality which would make motherhood impossible to the English Queen. But she was very conscious how closely she was "descended of the blood of England," and had no intention of waiving her rights as next in the royal succession. "We will deal frankly with you and wish that ye deal friendly with us," Mary protested; and for awhile she and Maitland and even Randolph seem to have believed the meeting would take place in the following spring. Ironically enough, Huntley and some of the remaining Scotch Catholics opposed their Queen's English visit as a possible danger to her faith — while the Protestants across the Channel dreaded Mary as an emissary of Rome!

During the late days of winter a strange drama played itself out, with Bothwell, Knox, and the young Earl of Arran as protagonists. Act I saw the indomitable Hepburn, back from his brief banishment, protesting sorrow for the scandal of his life and begging John Knox to bring about a reconciliation with Châtelheraut's son, so that the two might work together and — candidly — so that he might be freed of the extra expense of maintaining a constant bodyguard of "wicked and unprofitable men." Both ideas appealed to the preacher, whose hard heart always kept some atavistic softness for the Bothwell family; and as God's "public messenger of good tidings" he promised to unite the two Protestant earls in amity. He proved as good as his word — but the story was far from ended. Three days later Arran burst into Knox's study in a half-frenzied state, declaring he had been treasonably betrayed "by a Judas." When the preacher not unreasonably demanded a "less dark manner of speaking," the distraught heir of the Hamiltons confessed: "The Earl Bothwell has shown me in counsel that he shall take the Queen and put her in my hands in the Castle of Dumbarton; and that he shall slay the Earl of Mar, Lethington and others that now misguide her; and so shall I and he rule all." Whether such a conspiracy had actually been weighed between the two nobles — which everybody in Scotland knew to be quite possible — or whether the wish was father to the thought in Arran's obviously diseased mind, Knox could not tell. But the young man was apparently terrified that Bothwell would reveal the whole plot to the Queen, and was determined to do it first by sending her an immediate letter. In vain John Knox, who was as much of a politician as a preacher, warned the hysterical earl that if he had not consented to treason he could not be considered guilty — while he might easily excite suspicion by accusing Bothwell with no corroborating witness. The advice was quite useless. Arran rushed away, wrote out his confused confession to the Queen, and then sped off to join his father Châtelheraut; who promptly locked him up and threatened to put him to death!

Mary was at Falkland with Lord James and Maitland when Arran's letter arrived — followed closely by his cousin Gavin Hamilton, who announced that the suspect had already escaped by making a rope of his bedding, and that Châtelheraut and Bothwell both protested innocence of any share in his mad designs. It was a grave matter for everyone concerned. Mary knew, as her father had reason to know before her, that to kidnap their monarch was no new idea to the Scottish nobility. So the last act saw the Earl of Arran, who by this time was raving of "divels, witches and such like" — in which the Scotland of his time had a strong and perhaps not unjustified belief! — duly incarcerated for his real or assumed madness. Bothwell characteristically offered to prove his innocence by single combat, but was imprisoned in Edinburgh Castle. With his usual luck or skill he managed to escape; and although Mary refused to be reconciled, she was willing to wink at his flight to England and then to France. He was out of her way for the next two years, which saved complications where there were already quite enough. As epilogue the old, shifty Duke of Châtelheraut came to court, again affirming his innocence and weeping "like a chylde beaten." So of course Mary granted her pardon; although she took away from him that Dumbarton Castle which her mother had put into his keeping.

CHAPTER X

FALSE TURNINGS

IT SEEMS a curious fact that in the more or less continous discussions of Mary's marriage her powerful Protestant brother and her Protestant secretary, Maitland, seemed to favor the Catholic Spanish alliance with Don Carlos: curious, that is, if one forgets that such a union would probably have removed the Queen to Spain or Flanders, leaving Lord James's friends in full command with himself as Regent. This was the post to which he now aspired and toward which he assiduously worked, having given up his more youthful hope of wresting the crown itself from his royal sister's head.

The character of Lord James seems to have been the rather typical one of the resentful and ignoble royal bastard — just as that of his younger contemporary, Don John of Austria, illustrated the heroic side. From his father, the fortright if philandering James V, he inherited little except the instinct and some of the ability of leadership. With none of the Stuart charm, he brought from his mother the old Erskine pride with a complete abandonment of the old Erskine faith and loyalty. So, growing up with a mixture of what we now call the superiority and inferiority complex — a resentment that he, the eldest of James's children, should be barred from the throne — he developed extreme jealousy and a thirst for power and money which even the benefice of St. Andrews and the earldoms of Mar and Moray were insufficient to satisfy. In his Protestant allegiance he was probably sincere, for it offered at once a blow to the old legitimate order and new opportunities for individualism. But the legend of the "stainless Moray," built up for propaganda purposes, had about as much reality as the similar one of Gloriana, the Virgin Queen — who, by the by, so frequently used and rewarded him. He was extremely astute in sensing his sister's faulty judgment and tendency to lean on others. Wise in his generation, he determined to be the *power behind the throne:* and he developed a positive genius for providing alibis when the crimes he had abetted were consummated.

During all that spring of 1562 negotiations for a state meeting of Mary and Elizabeth continued. Almost everybody, including Mary's French uncles and her Scotch Privy Council, saw the advantages of it: the only serious obstacles being Lord Cecil's distrust and the increasing politico-religious tension in France between the Catholics led by de Guise and the Huguenots led by the Prince de Condé. To the Queen of Scots this was particularly distressing, for both personal and patriotic reasons, and many reports of her weeping over ill news are handed down. June, however, brought hopeful letters from Maitland and Elizabeth herself, which Mary welcomed with premature and somewhat extravagant joy. She immediately told Master Randolph the good tidings, protesting that "above all things" she desired to meet her sister Queen, to whom she was sending "a ring with a diamond shaped like a heart," accompanied by a "few verses," since nothing could better symbolize her good will. In July a pact was signed arranging a meeting of the two monarchs at York or some near-by spot between the approaching 20th of August and September: Mary to be permitted a train of one thousand persons, crossing the Border two hundred at a time, and to be assured freedom of worship while in England. She immediately began elaborate preparations — for her dramatic sense was always keen — when Elizabeth suddenly changed her mind, or had it changed for her. She was sending re-enforcements to the embattled Huguenots, doubtless with Cecil's approval, and postponed the meeting with her cousin until "the spring of the next year."

In the midst of these negotiations and counternegotiations, in which Mary tended to place excessive hope, another problem suddenly faced her: the arrival of Nicholas Goudanus or de Gouda as Papal envoy to Scotland. That Scotland needed such an apostolic ambassador was obvious — that she was not prepared to welcome one was soon equally clear. The position of Catholics was incredibly lamentable. The Scottish Church being composed of Scotchmen, had always tended to be more or less lawless.* More even than in Continental countries the custom of conferring benefices upon laymen — particularly the illegitimate sons of king or high nobles — had prevailed, with a consequent lowering of discipline and increase of worldly standards among religious houses and secular clergy. Then, instead of the needed reforms from within, came heresy, persecution, devastation, the usual loot among the nobility, and upon the death of Marie de Guise, the formal repudiation and dispossession of the Old Religion. After the murder of Cardinal Beaton, there was no Catholic leader capable of challenging the dynamic and fanatical John Knox.

To the reigning Pope, Pius IV (1559–1565), and his sainted successor Pius V (1566–1572), conditions in Scotland were a

----

* "In the 16th century its barons still belonged to the 12th, despite a thin veneer of French manners. . . . Nowhere else was there a seed-plot better prepared for revolutionary ideas of a religious sort." *Cambridge Modern History*, Vol. II.

cause of grief and alarm. Much — too much — was hoped
when young Mary Stuart returned to her kingdom; and as
practically nothing seemed to be accomplished in the first
year, the Holy Father decided to send the learned and holy
Dutch Jesuit, de Gouda, to report fully on the Church
situation, to urge Scottish bishops to attend the reconvened
Council of Trent and to strengthen the faith of the Queen
herself. It was a perilous mission. Father William Crichton,
a Scotch Jesuit, records that almost from the day de Gouda
arrived, accompanied by a French priest named Rivat, "the
heretical ministers knew about it and clamored in their pul-
pits that the Papal Antichrist had despatched an ambassador
to corrupt the Queen with his bribes and to destroy the
Gospel. 'Wherefore, let all true gospellers search for, capture
and slaughter that enemy of Christ.' " De Gouda, met and
harbored by another Scottish Jesuit, Father Edmund Hay,
was therefore immediately disguised "in court finery, with
top boots, a plumed hat and a sword swinging at his girdle."
Even so Mary seems to have been afraid to admit him in
audience and actually kept him waiting some six weeks —
an eloquent commentary on the degree of her subjection
to Lord James and the other Covenanting lords to whom she
had unwisely given so much leeway.

At last, on Sunday morning July 24th, while most of the
court were in attendance at St. Giles, Father de Gouda was
conducted with great secrecy to Holyrood House, accompanied by Fathers Rivat and Hay as interpreters in case
these should be needed. They were: for while the Queen
fully understood de Gouda's Latin, she explained apologeti-
cally that she "could not so easily reply to everything in that
language." It soon became apparent that the difficulties were
more than linguistic, and that the churchman was to be
thwarted at every turn. When he suggested an interview
with Lord James she gave no encouragement, nor could

she undertake any help in delivering to her bishops the
briefs inviting them to the Council of Trent. The establishment of seminaries to train the native clergy — one of the
prime points of Tridentine reform — was a dream she saw
no financial or practical way to accomplish. And while
expressing the rather pathetic hope that the Holy Father
would consider her will rather than her deeds of allegiance,
she admitted that if she gave the Nuncio letters of safe-con-
duct they would expose him to still greater danger; his only
safety lying in keeping to "some secret chamber" and getting
out of the country as soon as possible. The final mark of
Mary's humiliation was not lost upon the patient but vigilant Jesuit: all through the interview she kept watching the
door like a frightened child, in terror of being discovered
by her returning lords.

De Gouda went his saddened way, trying to reach the
scattered and somewhat skulking bishops as best he could,
but of Mary's apparent lack of zeal he took the large view.
"The leading men in her government acknowledge her
title but do not let her use her rights," he noted shrewdly
in his official report. And by her personal piety and good
will he seems to have been favorably impressed, since he
added that he *pitied* the "devout young gentlewoman, scarcely
twenty years old," standing "absolutely alone" without a
single Catholic adviser or protector. One is surprised by his
assertion that "even her confessor had left her" — it must
have been René Benoit — before de Gouda returned to
Flanders in September.

He had not left the country when Mary made one of the
first great errors of her queenly career. It all started innocently enough by an official visit to the Highlands, which
Lord James had been urging apparently as a sequel to her
expedition of the previous year. Bravely enough she and her
party set out — including a rather unwilling member in the

English Randolph. He was constantly amazed by Scottish
poverty and the dogged Scottish endurance shown even by
the Queen. "From Stirling she taketh her journey as far
north as Inverness, the fartherest part of Moray," he later
complained: "a terrible journey both for horse and man, the
countries are so poor and the victuals so scarce."

At Stirling there came an interruption from the ubiquitous
Master Knox, who broke in upon the party with an auda-
cious plea for the Privy Council to send aid to the French
Huguenots as Elizabeth of England was doing. But it seems
to have made small impression even upon Lord James. The
latter, some while before his recent marriage, had entered
into a betrothal contract with the young Countess of Buchan
— the orphan of a lord slain in battle, and so entitled to be
a ward of the crown until she could manage her own estate.
Quite unlawfully he had obtained the wardship of the lady
and her lands, lodging the girl with his mother at Lochleven
Castle. Now Buchan happened to lie close to the great estate
of Moray, then in the tenure of Huntley; and as Lord James
was determined to gain possession of both, this expedition
offered a politic method of killing two birds with one stone,
all with the Queen's apparent sanction. The fact that Huntley
had been cool to Mary's English visit, and that his son Lord
George Gordon had recently got into a typical Scottish
brawl in Edinburgh, later making a typical Scottish escape
from the Tolbooth, all played into Lord James's hand. It
was easy now for him to sow suspicion of treason in his
too credulous sister's mind. So when the Earl of Huntley —
having been warned to travel with only a hundred followers
— proudly rode up accompanied by fifteen hundred Highlanders, inviting the royal party to share the hospitality of
his magnificent estate at Strathbogie, Mary curtly refused
his invitation. By this time she ought to have realized the
feudal condition of Scotland, and to have accepted as her

father had the fact that the greater earls were practically kings within their own domains. She did no such thing: and of the blustering old Highland chieftain she made an enemy where she had every reason to find a friend.

At Inverness the whole sorry business came to a head. After turning down Huntley's invitation to Strathbogie — Randolph had accepted and found "his cheer marvellous great, his mind such as it ought to be towards his sovereign" — Lord James now advised his sister to lodge at the local Gordon stronghold, riding up and demanding entrance in the Queen's name. Whether the temporary keeper knew the Queen herself was in the group is uncertain: at any rate he refused to unlock the gates without orders from Lord Gordon, his superior and Huntley's heir. Technically this was treason; and although by the next morning the young man repented and sent out the keys, Lord James saw to it that he and several of his companions were promptly beheaded for their insolence. But by this time Mary was thoroughly persuaded the Gordons were fomenting rebellion. She sent to Edinburgh for re-enforcements — which arrived with suspicious haste, led by the Earl of Morton (Sir Edward Parry was convinced the whole quarrel had been engineered between Morton and Lord James before the expedition started out!), and there was a general gathering of the clans. It was Mary Stuart's first experience of actual battle, and she reacted with a verve and excitement amazing to at least one of her companions. "I never saw her merrier, never dismayed, nor even thought that stomach to be in her that I find," reports the watchful Randolph: adding that she had cried out to one of the returning watch her wish that she, too, might have been a man, "to know what life it was to lie all night in the fields" or to walk upon the causeway with helmet and broadsword!

To shorten a long and involved story, poor old arrogant Huntley was hopelessly outnumbered. His two younger sons,

Sir John and the boy Adam, were taken prisoner — the former too hastily executed — and he himself fell dead from his
captor's horse in an apoplectic stroke. Later his coffined body
was taken to Edinburgh; where according to a rather barbarous Scotch custom, it was stood upright in parliamentary
court and formally tried and condemned for treason. The
lands and title of Moray were now openly conferred upon
Lord James Stuart, while the post of High Chancellor of
Scotland went to his confederate, the Earl of Morton. The
impetuous Lord George Gordon, who had been the osten-
sible cause of the trouble, stripped of his honors and income,
was duly imprisoned, but saved by Mary's timely intervention from the death Lord James had planned.

So, at the end of a stormy November, the Queen returned
from her ill-starred pilgrimage, and immediately fell ill from
something that sounds like our modern influenza. When she
took up life again she was more tightly bound than ever in
the hands of her determined Protestant leaders. For she had
herself almost annihilated the hotheaded Catholic Gordons
— the one power strong enough to protect her in the days
ahead.

CHAPTER XI

THE EXPENDABLE QUEEN

AT MONTROSE, on the way back from that fateful Highland trip, the royal party was joined by what at the time seemed a cheerful addition. This was the young French poet and courtier, Pierre de Chastelard, who with Brantôme and the French uncles had been in the party accompanying Mary back to Scotland. He came now with letters of recommendation from her old friend and admirer Henri de Montmorency, the Sieur d'Anville, in whose family he had formerly been a page. Mary was of course aware how deeply the Montmorencys were involved in Huguenot activities, but her inclination was always toward tolerance; so, being badly in need of cheering up, she welcomed without question this ambassador of the French culture which was her second nature. Chastelard traced a left-handed descent from the celebrated Chevalier Bayard; he both wrote and recited poetry with grace and he was an accomplished dancer — all of which endeared him to the Queen and her other Marys. So he was soon quite at home, taken not too seriously but given royal encouragement and royal presents, as Mary had seen court poets treated in France. Whether the light-headed young man misunderstood these gestures and became deliriously infatuated with the Queen — as the romancers have liked to have it — or if more sinister motives influenced him from the first, will probably never be known. But late one night at Holyrood House, when Mary returned from a conference with her brother and Secretary Maitland, Chastelard was found hiding in the royal bedchamber. Somewhat lamely he expostulated that he had been waiting for an audience and fallen asleep: and it was decided to pardon him on condition that he leave Scotland at once.

Mary with part of her court proceeded then toward Fife. And a few nights later, as her tiring women prepared to leave her and the Queen was about to climb into her curtained bed, the poet — who had secretly followed them from Edinburgh — attempted to break into the room armed with a dagger. The screams of Mary and her ladies roused the guard, and within a few minutes the Earl of Moray (Lord James) appeared and had the Frenchman taken into custody. There was but one possible outcome for such an offense: it could not be twice condoned. So before February was out the reckless troubadour was tried at St. Andrews and promptly condemned. In true Renaissance fashion, he beautifully recited Ronsard's "Hymn to Death" before kneeling down beside the block.

Chastelard being a Protestant, John Knox had volunteered as chaplain; and it was he who later announced that the poet made "a godly confession" before the end — and who, with his usual evil mind, found suspicion in the fact that his last words had been "O cruelle Dame!" But Maitland himself hands down the information that this confession admitted the poet had been sent from France by certain high Huguenots — one being "Madame de Curosot," a mysterious cipher name for Coligny's wife — with the express purpose of involving Mary's reputation if not her honor, and so compromising her prospects of a favorable alliance. It seems unlikely that one so emotional and impractical had any part in the idea of betraying the Queen with whom he was undoubtedly infatuated. He was probably the dupe of those who used his melodramatic nature and then left him alone to pay the price. But after this episode, Mary Fleming was assigned to share the royal bedchamber.

Mary Stuart's nerves, naturally showing increased tension under this unhappy accumulation of events, had soon to bear another shock. In that same month of February, 1563, her French secretary suddenly arrived in full mourning to bring news of the assassination of her uncle, the Duc de Guise. This implacable and all-but-invincible soldier had been called back to command when Catherine de Medici began to fear the power of the Huguenots she had formerly encouraged, and he was fresh from his victories over them and the English when he was stabbed at Orléans by a young Calvinist, Poltrot de Méré. "Ah Jésu! Jésu!" cried the Scottish Queen, as this link with her proud and happy youth snapped so tragically. For days she wept: and the Earl of Moray, always easily roused to jealousy, complained that her grief, and that of her Marys who had known the gentler side of de Guise in France, was excessive. There are increasing stories of her illnesses at this time — the beginning of a "pain in the side" which became chronic, and periodic prostrations which compelled her to give audience to the English Randolph and others while lying in bed. Then rather quickly she would rise again and return doggedly to the royal routine. "God save that sweet face!" the women of Edinburgh cried out as their pale Queen rode smilingly by to open Parliament, "her robes upon her back and a rich crown upon her head." Perhaps the distraught Mary was a little comforted: but she probably was beginning to realize the small weight of power or affection, either, she could count upon.

As a marriage prospect, however, and possible mother of a male heir to the throne, she remained richly expendable to Scotland. She must often have been sick with weariness as the interminable negotiations wore on — negotiations in which the last thing considered was her own heart or her own happiness. For more than a year Maitland had been paying visits to London and having secret interviews (only too well known to the omnipresent English spies), with the Spanish ambassador, Don Alvaro de la Quadra, Bishop of Aquila, on the subject of Don Carlos. From time to time Elizabeth threatened Maitland that if there were a marriage with Philip's son, she would bar Mary from the English succession — which was rather surprising, since she had so far refused to admit the Scottish Queen's rights in that line. Still more astonishing was de la Quadra's report that on one occasion the unpredictable Elizabeth remarked that if Mary wished to marry "safely and happily" she had best choose an Englishman — actually suggesting the name of Lord Robert Dudley, "in whom nature had implanted so many graces that if *she* wished to marry she would prefer him to all the princes in the world." It was a ruse, of course: a bold bluff, designed partly to clear her own name of the persistent reports of an intrigue with Dudley and partly to protest her good will to Mary while delaying the latter's plans for a foreign marriage. The Spaniard met it with incredulity, the Scottish Secretary with sarcasm; but as a matter of fact Elizabeth repeated the proposition next year to Mary herself — somewhat to the embarrassment of Dudley, soon to be created Earl of Leicester.

Meanwhile Philip II seems to have been more and more impressed by the idea of the Queen of Scotland as a daughter-in-law, and sent as messenger one Luis de Paz to Edinburgh, to discuss the project confidentially but in detail. In spite of Maitland's precautions the news seeped through and immediately Knox was on the war path, warning the Scotch lords that if they permitted "an infidel (and all Papists are infidels)" to marry their Queen, they would "banish Christ from the country, and bring down God's vengeance and a plague upon themselves." It was too much for the already overwrought sovereign, who straightway sent for the preacher, declaring with tears that she had borne his "admonishing" and abuse of herself and her Guise uncles, and had even sought his favor "by all possible means," but would tolerate no attack upon her plans for a marriage. He protested with his usual arrogance that as a "profitable member" of the commonwealth he had a right to speak his mind. When it became evident that not only the Queen but Maitland and other Lords of the Congregation were anxious to be rid of him, Knox seems to have compensated his ego by reviling some of the ladies-in-waiting near by, croaking out that "this knave Death" would presently be upon them in spite of their pretty clothes, and the "frail worms busy with this flesh."

It is pleasant to remember that John Erskine of Dun, one of the Protestant members of that famous family, finding Mary weeping after this painful interview, tried to comfort her with praise of her "beauty and excellence," protesting that every prince in Europe might well seek her favor. Not long afterward, however, the friendly de la Quadra died in one of London's periodic plagues, and by the next year negotiations for the Spanish marriage were abandoned. During all this time Mary Stuart tried to hold intact the usual line of royal amusements as well as royal duties. She rode and hunted and practiced archery and learned the Scotch game of golf — her own French name of *cadet* for the boy attendants being perpetuated in our universal *caddie*. Almost hectically she played at cards and danced or embroidered, while "Seigneur Davie" could be counted upon to be ever ready with flute and voice and also with the direction of the periodic court masques. There is a charming story of how, on Twelfth Night, Mary revived the old French game of the Bean King's Festival; and when Mary Fleming, having extracted the bean from the cake, was elected queen for the night, her royal mistress decked her in jewels and cloth of silver — wearing herself a simple black gown, with the ring Elizabeth had sent as sole ornament. But those who watched saw an ever increasing depression settling upon their young Queen.

So came on the spring of 1564. In France the religious civil war had subsided for awhile, and both sides were busy drawing up peace terms which would remove the English whom they mutually distrusted. Up in Edinburgh on Palm Sunday John Knox attempted to pacify his own civil war by taking to himself as a new wife the sixteen-year-old Margaret Stuart — a connection of the royal house. And on April 23rd, across the Border at the little village of Stratford-on-Avon, there was born into a family strongly suspected of secret allegiance to the Old Religion a son named William Shakespeare.

CHAPTER XII

THE COMING OF DARNLEY

ELIZABETH's hypocritical urging of an English lord as husband for the Scottish Queen was destined to prove a boomerang. So repeatedly had Mary been warned to choose "some fit nobleman within the island, well affected to concord; but that no child of France, Spain or Austria would be acceptable" to England, that she became converted to the idea. She had failed in her negotiations with Don Carlos and even in a meeting with Elizabeth: surely the matter of her succession to the English throne was worth some compromise? And at just this psychological juncture the Countess of Lennox — who as daughter of Mary's grandmother, Margaret Tudor, by the latter's second marriage with Archibald Douglas, was her own half aunt and only second in her rights to the English crown — began a determined campaign in favor of her son's wooing. This son was, of course, Lord Henry Darnley, already popular at the English court, where Elizabeth playfully called him the "long lad" because of his height, although others mocked him as "handsome, beardless and lady-faced." His father, the Protestant Earl of Lennox had, it will be remembered, been banished from Scotland in Mary's childhood for treasonable dealings with England — where he subsequently made his home and where Lord Henry was born and educated. That

he had been brought up a Catholic by his mother, Lady
Lennox, who had been a favorite with Queen Mary Tudor
and managed to keep on fairly good terms with Queen
Elizabeth, was an added asset to the Scottish Queen. For
Mary had not been comfortable since de Gouda's fruitless
embassy: through her uncle the Cardinal of Lorraine she
had sent a letter protesting to the Holy Father her devotion
to the Catholic Church, and begging to know the decisions
of the Council of Trent that she might have them observed
in Scotland.

She was, in fact, in a particularly dangerous state of
frustration during that year of 1564. She was estranged from
her brother, the Earl of Moray, because of his discourage-
ment of any remarriage at all and his now frank suggestion
of himself as her successor on the throne. She was so disappointed with Maitland's ministrations that she appointed
a new ambassador to England — Sir Thomas Melville: who,
after several diplomatic interviews with Elizabeth, reported
that "ther was nather plain dealing, nor uprycht meaning,
but great dissimulation" at the English court — facts which
she must already have known all too well. Things now began
to move quickly. In September the Earl of Lennox returned
to Scotland after twenty years' absence: he was "relaxed fra
the process of our Sovereign Lady's horn" — that is to say,
from his official banishment — and by a lavish series of enter-
tainments began a general reconciliation with the other
Scottish lords, including his particular enemy, old Châtelheraut. And very pregnant of future events was the fact that
toward the end of the year Mary, having cause for dissatis-
faction with her French private secretary, replaced him by
the devoted Rizzio, "Seigneur Davie."

In the January of 1565 the Queen with her four Marys
and a few other companions escaped from court complications for a little holiday at St. Andrews on the coast. Ran-

dolph, the English envoy and gossip, was invited to come along — mainly because at that time there seemed to be a burgeoning romance between him and Mary Beaton, just as there was another between the recently widowed Maitland of Lethington and Mary Fleming. But all four of these royal handmaids declared their intention of not marrying until their Mistress set the example! During this little interlude of freedom — in a sense the last Mary Stuart was ever to know — Randolph tried to guide the talk into state channels. But the Queen would have none of it: smilingly she pushed aside his questions, pointing to the simplicity of her surroundings and bidding him "See how like a bourgeoise wife I live with my little troop!"

Meanwhile young Darnley had arrived in Scotland: and probably in order that he might watch developments, Moray invited both him and the Queen to be his guests at the Castle of Wemyss on the Firth of Forth. It is almost certain that the two half cousins had seen each other formally in France just after the death of François II. But this was the first real meeting of Mary the woman — she was in her twenty-third year! — and the tall blond courtier of twenty who came as an avowed suitor for her hand. He talked well, he danced even better, and the much-thwarted Queen of Scots became almost immediately infatuated. Her blindness in the reading of men was notorious: and when, after a visit to his father Lennox, the young man reappeared in Edinburgh, she declared he was "the properest and best proportioned long man that ever she had seen . . . well instructed for his youth in all honest and comely exercises." It was all natural enough — and pitiful enough. And for awhile Henry Darnley was intent upon winning everybody's friendship. He went with some of the Lords of the Congregation to hear Knox preach, but was disgusted when that fanatic railed an hour and a half beyond his usual time. And he

completely captivated Rizzio with assurances of his devotion
to the Catholic Church and to Mary. Apparently all that
was needed for the Queen's subjugation was for him to fall
ill — which he did in April with an absurd attack of measles.
Mary Stuart, always a good nurse, could not be kept from his
side. When he recovered, and spring blossomed through the
stones of Edinburgh, it was evident to everyone that the
Queen of Scots was in love. It was at once a first love and a
mature one — for there had been no passion in the gentle
affection for her boy-husband in France — and it vitalized
her in all ways. Freed from fear of her tutelary Lords she
ordered the Easter Mass at Holyrood celebrated with great
"triumph"; to the usual organ music adding that of trumpet,
fife, drums, and bagpipes. She even learned to be merry again,
and Randolph was shocked to see her and her handmaids, disguised as burgesses in good old Stuart fashion, collecting
alms upon the streets of the town for dinner at a public inn.
Mary was happy, even inebriated, and her mad years had
begun.

To Maitland, Moray, and Elizabeth all this was matter
of the gravest concern. The English Queen promptly imprisoned Lady Lennox in the Tower, sent word recalling
Darnley and his father to their English allegiance, and
dispatched Throckmorton — who had known the young Mary
well when she was Queen of France — to find "how farr
forward" the plans for a marriage had gone and what could
be done to stop them. Nothing could, of course. Mary
listened courteously to Throckmorton — no doubt she would
have listened courteously to Knox had he come again to
face her — but the most she would promise was a delay of
three months. "Let her not be offended with my marriage
no more than I am with hers," she wrote reasonably
enough of Elizabeth's interference: "for the rest I will abyde
such fortune as God will send me." In point of fact, she knew

the match was not disapproved by either Philip II of Spain
or Charles IX of France; and while her uncle the Cardinal
contemptuously described Darnley as a *gentil huteaudeau*
— or pretty coxcomb — he promised to secure the papal
dispensation needed because of their consanguinity.

There is a popular and melodramatic legend to the effect
that the impatient Mary and Darnley were privately married
in Rizzio's apartment — by a priest, but before the canonical
dispensation arrived — sometime in April, 1565. It cannot be
corroborated and seems most unlikely. For Mary Stuart was
not an imaginative person, except in her optimism, and
Lord Henry was too selfish to be romantic. By this time,
indeed, his head was so completely turned that nothing short
of public recognition as King-Consort would have satisfied
him. Already he was patronizing the lairds of Scotland, and
is said to have drawn his dagger upon the messenger who
announced that while Mary was ready to create him Earl
of Ross, she must wait before conferring the Dukedom of
Albany.

In this crisis Moray withdrew from the court and conspired
an uprising: there were even plans to abduct both the Queen
and her fiancé, but these miscarried; while the disapproving
Morton and Maitland seem to have stood on the sidelines
waiting. So David Rizzio, who quite sincerely gave Mary the
advice she wanted to hear, was made unofficial Secretary of
State. "David now worketh all" reported Randolph resent-
fully, and Melville counseled the Italian to be more cautious
and humble in his bearing. Perhaps poor "Davie's" head was
a little turned also by the favors and authority heaped upon
him. "If it were so it were a grievous fault" — and grievously
was Rizzio to answer for it!

It seems to have been on July 22nd that the Bishop of
Dunblane arrived from Rome with the dispensation, although some of the more sensational authorities would have

us believe it was still further delayed. At any rate the banns
were called in the Queen's chapel at Holyrood House and also
at St. Giles, while a public proclamation announced to
Edinburgh and the rest of the kingdom that as Mary Stuart
had decided "to take to herself as her husband Henry, Earl
of Ross and Albany, the said Henry was henceforth to be
designated King of Scotland." Then at six o'clock on Sunday
morning, July 29, 1565, the brief and fatal marriage was
performed in the royal chapel by Dean John Sinclair of
Restalrig. For some reason Darnley departed after kissing
the Queen and placing the three official rings on her finger,
while Mary knelt on through the Mass. Always punctilious
about dress, she was wearing the black velvet of a widowed
Queen of France; but after returning to her own chamber
she allowed her maids to lay aside the widow's weeds and
clothe her in gay apparel for the state dinner which followed.
The Earl of Morton was in attendance, and of course Darnley's father the Earl of Lennox, but apparently not Maitland; while the usually ubiquitous Randolph confesses that,
like "a currish or uncourteous carle," he refused his own
invitation. Bitterly conspicuous was the absence of the
bastard brother upon whom Mary had so imprudently heaped
both favors and responsibilities.

There was small time for honeymoon happiness, since
this same brother almost immediately plunged Scotland into
civil war. No longer veiling his personal pique and his personal ambition, Moray was at Ayr, where he gathered around
him Châtelheraut, Argyle, Kirkaldy of Grange, and other
discontented lords. Mary, seeing the need of quick and
radical action, recalled Bothwell — the best and most dependable fighter of them all — from France; and freed the imprisoned Lord George Gordon, Huntley's son, who returned
to his title and his allegiance with a notable lack of resentment. And to her people she sent out a proclamation warning

them "that forasmuch certain Rebels, who under cover of religion intended nothing but the trouble and subversion of the Commonwealth," were gathering in revolt, therefore she and her husband "charged all manner of men, under pain of life, lands and goods, to resort and meet their Majesties at Linlithgow, the 24 of August." The effect of Mary's directness, and the known fact that she had never persecuted any man for his faith — together with the still divided factions of the Scottish nobility — all worked in her favor. When the tall young Queen rode out of Edinburgh with a crimson and silver tunic over her armor, the even taller young King rather imprudently armed in gilt, they had less than a thousand soldiers: when she arrived at Glasgow these had increased to five thousand, with Huntley's faithful Highlanders and Moray's less faithful deserters constantly swelling the numbers. Lord James thought best to slip back to Edinburgh, where he was certain his small army would be augmented by other Lords of the Congregation, also the troops and money he had been led to expect from England. Nothing of the sort happened: and Knox disconsolately tells us that although "all such men as would receive wages for the defense of the glory of God" were offered "good pay" to report the next day at St. Giles, "none or few resorted unto them." In actual fact the two armies never met — for which reason the revolt is known as the Run About Raid. It seems to have been only Morton's treacherous tactics of deflecting the royal army into Fife that prevented the fleeing Moray being taken prisoner. But Mary was obviously both pursuer and victor. In October she, who had addressed so many bootless letters to the "Right Excellent, Right High and Mighty Princess, our dearest Sister and Cousin the Queen of England," could write with some show of authority: "Madame my Sister: I understand you are offended without just cause against the King my husband and myself; and what is worse,

your servants on the Border threaten to burn and plunder
our subjects who wish to aid us against our rebels. If it please
you to make your cause that of our traitors, which I cannot
believe, we shall be compelled not to conceal it from our
princely allies." That thrust struck home. For Elizabeth
was always fearful of seeming to aid subjects against their
princes, and at this time was particularly anxious not to
stir up any more trouble with France and Mary's brother-in-
law Charles IX. So when Moray arrived in England seeking
protection she received him coldly, forced him to deny before
the French ambassador that she had had any part in the
uprising, and barely allowed him enough to live on in
London.

CHAPTER XIII

RIZZIO THE SCAPEGOAT

Immediately after Moray's rebellion it seemed that the Queen's tenure of her Scottish throne had never been more secure. She had victoriously routed her enemies, both Scotch and English, with the support of her lords and people: unfortunately these friends were as fickle in good as her foes were constant in evil. Mary was soon to learn that it was easier to conquer than to win — or as we put it now-days, to win a war than to win a peace. It had not occurred to anyone before — except, perhaps, a few of the more distraught Knox fanatics — to fear Mary Stuart. But a Queen triumphant over her brother, capable of picking her own leaders and winning a civil war, became potentially formidable. She became formidable to England, to Protestantism, to the jealous Scotch barons, even to the vain and ambitious cad she had taken as husband. And so fear hardened into hate in all these hearts: the hearts of Elizabeth and Moray, of the Lords of the Congregation and the "long lad" who wanted to be a king. It is appalling to think of such currents of hate suddenly — or was it gradually? — directed toward that lonely woman of not quite twenty-three. They would demand a victim: in fact more than one victim. . . . And the first scapegoat to be sacrificed was David Rizzio.

The sacrifice did not come immediately, of course. It

was engineered from several quarters. Both Maitland and Moray — the latter still in England — had been close to treason and were far from comfortable: also they were furiously jealous as they saw, after the revolt, their military authority taken over by Bothwell and their civil influence by Seigneur Davie. And about this same time the Scotch Protestants were warned that Mary was about to give them the treatment they richly deserved. She was not, never having the least inclination toward bigotry or persecution; although, with hoped-for financial help from the Pope and Philip II, she probably did contemplate restoring the devastated shrines and even re-establishing the Mass in her country. All these rumors were exaggerated when a confidential messenger from her uncle, the Cardinal of Lorraine, arrived to visit her — evidently for the purpose of discussing the future of Moray and his rebel friends. Now Master Randolph had been behaving badly through the whole rebellion: he was found to have handed over three thousand English pounds to the insurgents, and Mary was soon to ask his recall by England. But one of his worst acts before leaving Scotland was to propagandize the myth of the "Papal League." This imaginary union of Catholic sovereigns to stamp out Protestantism never really existed, for the reason that the various Catholic monarchs were then, as they had been during the Crusades, too divided by selfish national interests to agree upon any common action. If the Church was saved from extinction after the tragic break of the sixteenth century, it was, under God, through the reforms of the Council of Trent, through the dynamic zeal of St. Ignatius and the winning spirituality of St. Francis de Sales. But the League was believed in fearfully by many Protestants: it was even believed in hopefully by some Catholics. And in Scotland it was easy to add the conviction that Rizzio was a Papal agent. From this time on personal calumnies against the Queen of Scots also became part of the campaign: those calumnies which from Knox's sermons or Randolph's whispers spread to the populace, later reaching their peak of infamy in the *Detectio* gotten up by her Latin teacher, Buchanan, when she was imprisoned and he had passed over to the pay of Moray and the other usurping lords.

But bitterest of all, because closest to the woman's heart, was the behavior of her bridegroom. Less than three months after the wedding Randolph had informed Cecil that Darnley had made himself so detested, many of the Scotch lords were already determined upon his death. And because this English envoy was now alienated from the Queen, his testimony about Darnley to the Earl of Leicester is all the more credible: "All honor that may be attributed unto any man by his wife, he hath it wholly and fully, all praise that may be spoken of him he lacketh not from herself, all dignities that she can endue him with are already given and granted. No man pleaseth her that contenteth not him." And with somewhat heavy humor, Randolph closes with the remark: "She can as much prevail with him in anything that is against his will, as your Lordship may with me persuade that I should hang myself."

Undoubtedly Mary had for awhile been blindly in love, but she was not one to remain blind. Darnley's resentment over the crown matrimonial, which she had been willing to grant but the Scottish Estates had refused to ratify, was one eye opener. His increasing jealousy of anyone in royal favor — of Bothwell and Rizzio, later on of Moray and even of her women companions — was another. When she tried to curb his excessive drinking at an official dinner, he became so insulting that she left in tears. And after the coming of his disreputable uncle, George Douglas — an illegitimate brother of Lady Lennox, known as the Postulate because of some earlier connection with the Church from which he had fallen away — the evil of his life deepened. By New Year Mary knew that she had married a dissolute drunkard familiar with the night dives of Edinburgh, a jealous and ambitious egoist who would not hesitate to play with treason and murder. She also knew that she was to bear him a child. It is said that Rizzio, who had so unwisely urged her marriage with the "long lad," dared now to protest the latter's treatment of his royal wife. If so, he signed his own death-warrant. Darnley, already incensed by his elimination from State affairs, now began to believe — or pretended to believe — in a liaison between the proud and beautiful Queen and her deformed but devoted secretary.

Meanwhile Moray and the other exiled lords in England were making every effort to return to their Scotch possessions. Anybody who knew Mary must have realized that she would end by pardoning her brother: but the latter took no chances. He had his cause urged by the English Throckmorton, and sent a canny plea to Rizzio, enclosing a diamond peace offering, to hurry matters up. Then what might so easily have been accomplished by persuasion they determined to achieve by force — the hidden force of a "band" or conspiracy which would secretly include the death of the Queen's secretary. There were, in fact, two of these bands or deeds — copies are still extant — one signed by the banished Lords of Moray, Argyle, Glencairn, Ochiltree (Knox's new father-in-law), and others, promising the "mighty Prince Henry, King of Scotland" to "support him in all his lawful and just actions, to be friends to his friends and enemies to his enemies" — to "consent to his getting the Crown Matrimonial for life" with the right of succession, to maintain the religious situation as established by the Queen after her arrival, *etc., etc.* In the other bond Darnley ("Henry R.") swore to obtain the restoration of their lands and rights, to support them in the exercise of the reformed religion and to "maintain them as a good master should." It was all very obscure: but all those signing and a good many others knew perfectly what it meant. Morton was head and front of the conspiracy. Maitland's name does not appear, but a very suspicious letter from him to Cecil warns of coming events and declares that there will be no way out "unless we strike at the very root." And a later note from Randolph to Elizabeth's Treasurer mentions among "such as were consenting to the death of David" the names of "John Knox and John Craig, preachers." Obviously the plot was well known in English official circles; in fact, almost everyone seems to have known what was going to happen except Mary Stuart and her confidential advisers. Evidently she had no secret police and was weak on espionage. So, innocently enough, she rode along the Tolbooth on March 7th to open her Parliament — Darnley having peevishly refused to attend unless he could open it himself as "Sovereign of Scotland" — and a committee was duly appointed to hear Moray and the other banished lords the following week.

The next day Darnley played tennis with Rizzio at Holyrood, and there had been some talk of assassinating the always unarmed Italian at that time. On Saturday evening, March 9th, Seigneur Davie was one of an informal supper party in the Queen's apartment, along with her relative, the Countess of Argyle, Arthur Erskine, and a few others. After the meal, Rizzio is said to have been singing an old French air when Darnley suddenly entered through the tapestried door. Judas-like, he advanced and kissed Mary's throat; and with her usual courtesy she inquired whether he had yet supped. Then in the same doorway appeared the Earl of Ruthven — he was reputed to be a sorcerer and had once given the Queen a ring supposed to ward off poison — in armor and with drawn sword, closely followed by the sinister George Douglas and several of his armed retainers. When

Ruthven lifted his bony hand and ordered Davie to follow him from the room, Mary rose up between them, declaring, "It is by my will he is here." She then demanded of Darnley what he knew of the business, reminding him of Rizzio's good offices; but he was already half inarticulate by fear or liquor.

Arthur Erskine, long Captain of the Royal Guard, broke forward to eject Ruthven; but the door leading to Mary's bedroom was broken down from the outside and the Earls of Morton and Lindsay led a company of armed ruffians into the supper chamber. The table was overturned with its china and glass, and if the Countess of Argyle had not seized one of the candelabra as it fell to the floor the room would have been in darkness. Darkness, indeed, would have become the following scene, for it was one of the most hideous in history. Crouching on the floor behind Mary's full skirts, the helpless Rizzio cried out in his native tongue for *"Giustizia, giustizia!"* — as though he did not know how little *justice* was to be found in Scotland . . . . His last words, as she tried vainly to protect him, went into the plea *"Sauve ma vie, Madame!"* Then one of the so-called nobles held a cocked pistol to the side of his Queen, while George Douglas reached across her shoulder to drive his dagger into Rizzio's back. It was the first of fifty-six thrusts, as the Scotch lords, inflamed by blood-lust, dragged the bleeding Davie through her bedroom and finally threw him down the narrow stairway leading to Darnley's apartment.

The horror of it all froze Mary at first into a strange composure. With true intuition she faced her husband, demanding: "My Lord, what offense have I given that you should do me such shame?"

His answer was rambling but characteristic. "Since yonder fellow David came into credit and familiarity" with her Majesty — did he forget how long that credit antedated his own, and how willingly it had been used to forward his marriage with the Queen? — she had "neither regarded him, entertained him, nor trusted him after her wonted fashion." Nor had she made him her "equal in all things," nor come to his chamber before dinner, but was "coy with him at all times alike." In this frightful moment Darnley fell back upon the only things that mattered much to him, power and sex.

Mary understood him all too well. And as she began to understand the depths of treason and infamy which had led to this night's work a tempest of tears broke her. "My Lord," she cried half hysterically, "all the offense that is done me, you have the wit thereof, for the which I shall be your wife no longer, nor lie with you any more, and I shall never like well till I cause you as sorrowful a heart as I have at this present."

Almost at that moment came another knocking at the door, and Ruthven opened to admit Bothwell, young Huntley, Maitland, and a group of the Queen's professed followers. Then he told them, showing the false King's name upon the band, that the murder had been done upon Darnley's consent and suggestion; adding that Moray and his revolting lords had been given permission to return and would reach Edinburgh the following day. Perhaps some lightning flash of comprehension — some tardy realization that here was a coup d'état to supplant the Queen as well as a conspiracy to kill Rizzio — passed between Mary and Bothwell, the commanding officer of her army and navy. At any rate he made an unexpectedly wise move. Seeing the courtyard full of armed enemies and comprehending that she was already a prisoner, he and Huntley withdrew quietly and posted off to prepare for her rescue. After all, something could be left to the wit of Mary Stuart.

Never had this wit been keener than in that zero hour

when the Queen realized how close she and her unborn child were to death or captivity. Having looked upon the murder of her faithful friend and the perfidy of her most unfaithful husband, she herself had little left to lose. But for her heir there was everything to lose or to gain. And through the lonely, sleepless hours in her blood-stained bedroom — from which even her ladies-in-waiting were barred — the immemorial instinct of motherhood rose to possess and inspire her, conquering the lethargy of grief and exhaustion. She who, as Queen of France, had scorned to seek any favors, became now as wise as the serpent, as winsome as the stray dog or cat hunting a home where its young may be born. Probably there was not much dissimulation when, the next day, Mary fell into the arms of her returning brother, protesting, "If you had been here, you would not have allowed me to be so cruelly treated": for by this time his crime of opposing the Darnley marriage did not seem very heinous. But this trustfulness, together with her obvious illness — she was in the sixth month of her pregnancy and had come through an inhuman ordeal — was not a little disarming. Even while he planned the Queen's banishment to Stirling or Lochleven, Lord James consented to clear Holyrood House of the offending guards and to permit Mary Livingston to attend his sister.

With the vacillating Darnley, Mary was equally successful. When he appeared with a new "band" promising pardon to Rizzio's murderers, she wisely deferred her signature; meanwhile persuading him that he would probably be the next victim of their brutal jealousy (he was already feeling their snubs!), and that his only safety lay in immediate flight with her to Dunbar Castle. It was a daring and dangerous chance; but Mary had somehow smuggled out word to her few trusty ones, and she knew that her spirit could spur the poor body on to the thirty-mile ride. So on Monday about midnight she and her now docile husband slipped out from his apartment into the old Abbey cemetery, where her Captain, Arthur Erskine, was waiting with horses. Keeping close to the shadows to avoid the moonlight, Darnley's mount slipped ominously over Rizzo's freshly made grave; and — whether from remorse or hypocrisy, who can tell? — he cried out: "Poor Davie, every day of my life I shall regret him! I have been miserably cheated." . . . But Mary only whispered, "Poor David, my good and faithful servant — may the Lord have mercy on your soul!" Choking back her tears she pressed on.

Outside of Seaton other horsemen appeared ahead, and the timorous Darnley tried to urge Mary's horse into a gallop. Really suffering now and in fear of a miscarriage, she protested she would risk any chance rather than imperil the life of her child. But her husband, sinking back into his old brutal egotism, persisted: "In God's name come on! If this baby dies we can have another."

It was just the final disenchantment for the Queen of Scots. "Push on then, and take care of yourself!" she ordered — which he promptly did.

But the horsemen proved to be Bothwell's outriders sent to meet her: and it was with the Earls of Bothwell, Huntley, Fleming, Seaton, and Livingston that she finally reached Dunbar and safety.

CHAPTER XIV

THE HEIR AND WHAT HE BROUGHT

B‌EFORE the end of March the same lords, accompanied by some 3000 troops they had hastily raised, brought Mary and Darnley back to Edinburgh in another temporary triumph. Not wishing to return to her memory-stained apartment at Holyrood House, she moved into a transient lodging in High Street. And one of her first preoccupations was to reconcile her brother, Moray, and her new champion the Earl of Bothwell. The two touched hands and swore amity; and the *entente cordiale* lasted about as long as such forced friendships usually do. Master Knox had gotten out of town shortly after the Rizzio affair — some say to Ayrshire, some across the Border. And as Morton was still in banishment, the Queen appointed George Gordon, the young Earl of Huntley, to the post of Chancellor formerly held by his father. The Privy Council heard Darnley's protestation of complete innocence in the plot — it was posted at the market cross with rather suspicious publicity — and ordered Morton, Ruthven, and about sixty others to appear and defend themselves. But in spite of the wise urgency of Mary's Catholic friends and of churchmen abroad that she should see justice done upon the assassins, nothing adequate was ever accomplished. Probably the woman was weary of the intricate story of hate and treason, crime and revenge.

As the time for her *accouchement* drew near the Queen was transferred to Edinburgh Castle for greater security. Evidently anticipating her possible death in childbirth, she made a will in which at least two clauses stand out. In the first, with a public spirit unusual at the time and under the circumstances, she bequeathed the "Great Harry," finest of the crown diamonds, to the kingdom of Scotland. In the second she left to Darnley a certain diamond set in red enamel, with the words: "It was with this ring I was married. I leave it to the King who gave it to me."

But Mary Stuart was not to die so easily. On Wednesday morning, June 19th, 1566, Mary Beaton came from the royal bedchamber announcing the happy birth of a son: and the city's cannon and churchbells competed with one another to celebrate. A few hours later, when her husband came to see the infant, Mary looked up at him from her pillows. "My lord, God has given you and me a son," she breathed weakly. Then the memory of all the ignoble calumnies which Darnley himself seems to have forgotten swept upon her, and Lord Herries reports that she raised her voice: "I protest to God, as I shall answer to Him at the great day of judgment, this is your son and no other man's son. And I am desirous that all here, both ladies and others, bear witness: for he is so much your son that I fear it will be the worse for him hereafter. . . ."

Her eyes closed from exhaustion, but a moment after this cryptic prophecy she gathered strength to utter what was to be for better or worse the *leitmotif* of her future life: "This is the son who, I hope, shall first unite the kingdoms of Scotland and England."

"Madame, shall he succeed before your Majesty and his father?" demanded a courtier standing by.

Mary wept easily, as a rule; but we are told of no tears as she answered, "His father has broken to me. . . ."

At last Darnley, incapable of any deep emotion, spoke up: "Sweet Madame, is this your promise that you made to forgive all and forget all?"

"I have forgiven all," replied Mary, "but I will never forget."

"Madame, these things are all past," he protested lamely.

"Then let them go," answered the Queen who was still in the Debatable Land between Life and Death.

And from the silence of the crowded room her husband made his shamed exit: hurrying away to write King Charles IX of France, begging him to stand sponsor for the baby — and so "increase the debt of gratitude" he, Darnley, owed him "for all his favors."

Meanwhile the Scottish Melville was posting to England with the news that was to mean so much for both countries. Elizabeth, who had just come through a serious illness, listened with mixed emotions, for she suspected the child was her own heir as well as Mary Stuart's. There was pathos and bitterness, too, in her historic comment: "The Queen of Scots is mother to a fair son, while I am but a barren stock!" But even yet she would give no direct promise about the succession.

Mary did not recover quickly — perhaps she would have been glad not to recover at all. But in about a month, when the royal baby was installed at Stirling Castle with the nurse, Lady Reres, the cradle-rockers, and various other attendants, she slipped quietly away from the grim fortress-castle where her mother had died, to recuperate at the country seat of the new Earl of Mar — Sir John Erskine, also custodian of Edinburgh Castle — on the Firth of Forth. To reach there it was necessary to ride to Newhaven and there take ship for Alloa. The ship — like all the others of her small navy

— was serviced by Bothwell's men, since he was High Admiral of Scotland. Those who throve on slandering the Queen later on did not hesitate to take scandal from this occurrence, as from the equally innocent fact that at Alloa she was entertained by the far-from-exciting masques and dances of the day. The mother of the heir was no longer expendable — she was even becoming superfluous!

Upon her return to Holyrood, Darnley's growing jealousy of Moray took a dangerous turn, and Mary was obliged to warn her half brother of the "long lad's" threat to kill him. It must have been about this time, too, that her husband began his treasonous correspondence with Charles of France, Philip of Spain, the Cardinal of Lorraine, and even Pope Pius V, warning them that the Queen was "dubious in the Faith" and suggesting himself as Catholic champion of Scotland! This Mary can scarcely have known as yet: what she did know from the message of his father, Lennox, was that Darnley was on the point of setting out secretly for France. With characteristic directness she sent for him and demanded the cause of such action. It is probable that what he feared was that if Mary pardoned Rizzio's murderers — as she probably would — they might conspire against him for his perfidy. He would not admit this, of course; but he was compelled to bear public witness before the lords that he had no cause for complaint against the Queen's treatment. In this same month of September Mary was reconciled with Maitland of Lethington, whom she reinstated — against Bothwell's advice — in his old post of Secretary of State.

In October, when the Queen went to Jedburgh to preside at the important Border assizes, she was met by news of another casualty. Bothwell, her indomitable commander of that turbulent country, had been set upon by a highwayman and so dangerously wounded that he was first reported dead. Mary had food and supplies sent to his castle, the Hermitage;

and a week later, after the assizes were finished, she rode over to see him, accompanied as usual by Moray and Maitland. In the party also was young Huntley, whose sister Lady Jean Gordon, had — with Mary's approval — been married to the philandering Earl shortly before Rizzio's murder. They found him laid low, with one arm broken and his head and body heavily bandaged: altogether in such a bad state that a few days later he was carried back to Jedburgh for better attention. It would be vastly interesting to know just what were the feelings of the Queen at this time toward her selfish, swaggering, but intensely loyal champion. At first — in spite of the fact that he and his father, the old Earl Patrick Hepburn, had been faithful supporters of Marie de Guise and incorruptible by English bribes — she had disapproved of Bothwell because of his questionable reputation and generally lawless speech and behavior. When he rose to her aid so powerfully during Moray's rebellion and again after the Rizzio assassination, she was naturally filled with gratitude and rewarded him with the Border command and the restoration of his hereditary title of Grand Admiral of Scotland. But apparently she did not yet listen seriously to his advice, as she had coaxed or forced his acceptance of Moray and Maitland's return. Into her bitter disillusion with Darnley — the very thought of whom had now become, in Maitland's perceptive words, "an heartbreak" to her — admiration for her protector would inevitably obtrude. And with Mary, always pitifully responsive to illness, tenderness would now as inevitably follow. Nature has a way of bending us to her purposes, and Satan is almost as ingenious as God in catching us unawares! But if the harassed young Queen, awakened by her unhappy marriage and aware at last of her highly sensed Stuart heritage, suspected the danger of this not-impossible new passion, her Catholic ideals must have plunged her into an intense emotional conflict.

This seems to be exactly what happened during the innocent but ominous stay at Jedburgh. Superb horsewoman that she was, the long ride to Hermitage and back was too much for her weakened condition; and almost immediately after the invalid Earl's arrival, she herself fell ill of fever and presently could neither eat, speak, nor move. That she was near death seemed evident, and for several hours she actually appeared dead: "all her members cold, eyes closed, mouth fast and feet and arms stiff," as her old friend Bishop John Leslie wrote to her French ambassador Beaton. So far as can be judged today, it was an acute return of the psychosomatic symptoms which had pursued her ever since girlhood — a semihysterical attack close to catalepsy but still closer to what we now call shellshock. Modern psychiatry would suggest a subconscious wish to escape from life: understandable enough, since Mary Stuart's life had for more than a year been an almost unbroken story of shock, sorrow, humiliation, and illness. But her sixteenth-century French physician treated it quite objectively, rousing the circulation by massage and localized ligatures, forcing wine between her lips, etc.; and he did succeed in bringing her out of the long coma. Hemorrhage and other swoons followed, however, and Mary believed herself dying. Like her mother she called her lords about her (there was no priest at hand!), reminding them that "by discord all good purposes are brought to naught" and begging Moray "not to be over-extreme to such as were of her religion." Then she forgave all her enemies — including Darnley, who had snatched a few hours to visit her and then hurried away — and commended her baby son to his royal godparents, Charles of France and Elizabeth of England.

But again Mary's vitality triumphed, and by the middle of November she was able to stand the journey back to Edinburgh. On the way she stopped at Craigmillar Castle for a conference with the Earls of Moray, Maitland, Bothwell (unusually silent and still with bandaged head), Huntley, and Argyle. The approaching baptism of the prince was one subject of discussion, another was the return of Morton and his banished companions. But as usual the real problem was Darnley, whose treasonable efforts against the Queen were now discovered. "He troubles your Grace and us all," began Maitland persuasively; "and if he remains with your Majesty he will not cease until he does you some evil turn, which your Highness will be much hindered to remedy." His own suggestion was divorce and banishment for her husband, with possibly trial for high treason. The Queen listened carefully, even wistfully: longing to be rid of Darnley but hating the idea of even a legal divorcement. At first she used the argument of possible complications to their son and heir, but these were quickly swept aside by Bothwell — himself the child of divorced parents.

The harassed woman turned wearily from this new temptation. "I will that you do nothing by which any spot may be laid to my honor or conscience," she insisted, "and therefore I pray you let the matter be . . . abiding till God of His goodness put remedy thereto."

No such pious solution was likely to appeal to the group before her. Maitland threw out a cryptic remark to the effect that the Earl of Moray — who was "little less scrupulous for a Protestant than your Grace is for a Papist" — would "look through his fingers" while the lords of her Council found a way out of the impasse. "Madame," he concluded suavely, "let us guide the matter amongst us, and your Grace shall see nothing but good and approved by Parliament."

After that the Queen threw what strength she had into preparations for the christening of her son on December 17th. The ceremony was to take place at Stirling Castle, where she herself had been crowned at almost the same age: and Mary, who had perhaps made too many concessions about her own religion, was determined to make none at all where her heir was concerned. So, much to the scandal of the absent Knox's followers, the royal baptism was the most elaborate Catholic pageant in Scotland since the Church had been repudiated. Mary and the official party, carrying lighted tapers, marched to the chapel, where the Comte de Brienne — representing the godfather, Charles IX — held the infant upon his velvet cushion. Queen Elizabeth, the godmother,* had sent a font of gold and deputed the Countess of Argyle to be her proxy — for which service that lady was later duly reprimanded by the Scottish Kirk. Bishop Hamilton, a left-handed brother of Châtelheraut, administered the sacrament to the little Charles James Stuart, assisted by the Bishops of Dunblane and Dunkeld. In a sense it was the vindication of Mary's Catholicity: and although Darnley petulantly refused to attend, and Moray and Bothwell — richly appareled, the one in red, the other in blue — stood with the other Protestant lords just outside the chapel door, she was almost happy. After the ceremony was over, all joined in a State banquet, served "at a round table, like Arthur's," followed by the usual music and masques, with fireworks outside for the delight of the villagers. Du Croc, the very understanding French ambassador, reports that the Queen in her gracious care for everyone almost forgot her persistent illness. But a few days later he adds that he fears a return: "Nor can I think otherwise, so long as she continues to be so pensive and melancholy." Of her husband, Darnley, he sums up the general impression: "His bad deportment is incurable, nor can there be any good expected of him."

----

* No doubt in the hope of winning back England to the Faith, Pope Pius V did not formally excommunicate Queen Elizabeth until 1570.

CHAPTER XV

THE DOOM OF DARNLEY

T HERE is probably no tragedy in history more understandable than the murder of King Henry Darnley. And yet to this day most of the details are highly debatable. His single excuse was, as he reminded Mary at one of their last interviews, his youth. But in less than twenty-three years he had found time to play fast and loose with his father, his friends, his wife and Queen, his infant son, the countries of his birth and his adoption, and his Church. And he had played badly. In almost any land and any age the wages of such a performance are likely to be death: in sixteenth-century Scotland such a climax was so inevitable that it had been predicted almost from the day of his marriage to Mary Stuart. Finally even she seems to have suspected the writing on the wall, for she was as careful as Darnley himself to track down rumors of plots against his safety. But in every case nothing but denials were forthcoming. In fact the rumors of Darnley's plots against her were far more convincing than any rumors of the "long lad's" own danger: although after the return of the Rizzio conspirators whom he had betrayed he had good reason to expect reprisals. For on Christmas Eve Mary had pardoned, at the urgency of the other advising lords, all the assassins and "accessories," except the Douglas who had first stabbed her secretary and the Fauldonside who had threatened her own life with his pistol.

In this atmosphere of doubt and fear Darnley decided to seek asylum with his father, the Earl of Lennox, in Glasgow. His health was by this time much undermined by his various excesses, and scientists tracing back the young man's symptoms suggest that he had already contracted syphilis. He certainly contracted almost everything else; and on the way to Glasgow — it is sad to remember that he had just started a new conspiracy to betray Mary, kidnap the baby prince, and have himself appointed Regent — he fell victim to the always prevalent smallpox. The Queen herself was still in fragile health and had been unable to attend the wedding of her cousin, Mary Fleming, to Maitland of Lethington on Twelfth Night. But when reports of Darnley's latest activities reached the court it was decided that she should leave the infant Charles James safely at Stirling awhile longer, and bring her husband back to Edinburgh where he could be better watched. So, late in January, she set out for Glasgow with a few servants, taking a horse-litter for Darnley's return. She found him almost recovered, although his face was still covered by a "taffetas mask"; but at first both he and his father strenuously objected to any movement. Mary coaxed and urged: he, as usual, excusing his offenses on the ground of "lack of counsel," and harping upon his return to political favor and hers to conjugal duties. Mary temporized, insisting first upon his complete recovery or "cleansing." It was a short and crowded visit, during which she was under constant surveillance by the Lennox household: but during this stay the Queen is supposed to have written three or four of the fatuous and compromising epistles to Bothwell — all, of course, without address or signature! — later produced among the so-called Casket Letters at her first trial in England. If it were possible to believe one of these letters, she also spent considerable time working upon a bracelet for her lover — which he was charged never to wear in public, as it would be recognized by others! What really happened was that, by the end of the week, the Queen had persuaded Darnley to return with her; and since he did not wish to go to Craigmillar as she suggested, and it was important for the baby's sake not to run the risk of contaminating Holyrood, the choice of his temporary lodging fell upon the Old Provost's House of Kirk o' Fields, part of the abandoned collegiate foundation of St. Mary on the south side of Edinburgh. Whether this choice was Darnley's own or Maitland's is still uncertain, but it was not so strange a location as some commentators have hinted. The air was purer than within the city, the residence of Bishop Hamilton was near by, and the New Provost's House was occupied by Sir James and Robert Balfour, courtiers who seem to have been considered friends of the vacillating King. Mary had some of the fine furnishings taken from Huntley's show-place at Strathbogie installed in Darnley's domicile, and she herself spent several days and nights there, sleeping on the first floor while her husband and his servants used the second. There was an adjoining *salle* or reception room, and here the various lords gathered when they came to visit the royal invalid.

Meanwhile the plot for the destruction of Darnley — and, there now seems good reason to believe, of Mary Stuart also — reached its head. On Sunday evening, February 9th, she was still at Kirk o' Fields, while the Earls of Bothwell, Huntley, Cassillis, Argyle, and others were playing dice with Darnley in the *salle*. About half past ten the lords rose to accompany the Queen, who had promised to return to Holyrood House for the marriage supper of her servant Bastian and Christine Hogg; leaving Darnley with his own valets. He was feeling so much better that, as the party left, he ordered his own horse for five o'clock the following morning. It is also reported that he had heard Mass — one hopes with good dispositions! — privately celebrated that very Sunday.

As Mary came out of the door to mount her horse, she is said to have noticed one of Bothwell's confidential servants about to enter with mysteriously blackened face, and to have cried out impulsively, "Jesu, Paris, how begrimed you are!"

Now the supposition is that he was "begrimed" because he had been moving bags of gunpowder into the cellar under the house, and that the Queen knew all about this criminal project. In point of fact her exclamation is its own defense. For it is as incredible that anyone cognizant of a secret gunpowder plot should have drawn attention to Paris' highly suspicious conduct, as it is impossible to believe that a woman of Mary Stuart's caliber should have been guilty of betraying — even of luring — Darnley to so hideous a death. The only sense in which the Queen can be considered at all responsible was in her refusal to allow him to be legally imprisoned or even impeached for high treason, or again in her too great lenience in pardoning the murderers of Rizzio. And both of these acts are chargeable to natural clemency and political ineptitude.

The few indubitable facts of that mysterious night are that Mary and her escort rode back to Holyrood for the wedding party, after which she retired to her own chamber, was undressed by her ladies, and presumably fell into a weary sleep. It was about 2 a.m. on February 10th that Edinburgh and its citizens — the guilty and the innocent — were shaken by a terrific explosion from the south side of the city. Before long came messengers with word that Darnley's dwelling at Kirk o' Fields was a wreck and he himself dead. Even here the story has unexplained and seemingly unnecessary complications. For the wretched young prince had not been killed by the explosion, as historians of the time reported and insisted upon handing down. According to several witnesses his half-clothed body and that of his servant Taylor

were found in the adjoining orchard, bearing no marks of
gunpowder at all but upon both throats the marks of
strangling. Evidently they had been wakened by suspicious
sounds or actions and had hastily escaped from the house
before the explosion — being followed into the garden or
orchard by some of the assassins and there dispatched.

Who the conspirators were it is not particularly hard to
surmise; althought practically all of the Scotch nobility, both
Protestant and Catholic, would have welcomed Darnley's
death as an act of justice if not of God. But the evidence does
narrow down. Moray's sudden departure from Edinburgh
on the plea of his wife's illness the Sunday before the murder
was running suspiciously true to form. So was the secrecy
with which Bothwell and Maitland, the former followed by
half a hundred hackbuteers, were seen riding about the streets
of Edinburgh. And Morton's participation was so generally
accepted that he was actually tried and executed for the
crime years later — when Mary Stuart was herself imprisoned in England and he had fallen from political favor.
In France the plot was always considered an invention of
the Scottish Protestant lords who would profit by it, with
possible encouragement from England. On the other hand,
a fantastic theory worked out in the last century by Major
General Mahon suggests that some fanatical Catholic party
at home or abroad, believing the Queen not zealous enough
in defending the Old Faith, had decided to make her its
victim and place her husband on the throne. But who among
the scattered Catholics would be strong enough or silly
enough to launch such a conspiracy — except the invalid
Darnley himself — has never been satisfactorily explained.

The most probable surmise is that the plot was originally
directed against both Darnley and the Queen by the triumvirate — Moray, Morton, and Maitland — who were eager
to take over the rule of Scotland; and that their confederate,

the dynamic Bothwell, saved Mary by making sure it was executed during her absence at Holyrood instead of during one of her many visits to Kirk o' Fields. It is unlikely that Mary realized as yet how high and how close to the throne the assassins stood: but in her letter to Archbishop Beaton in Paris, written the day after the murder, she assures him the conspiracy was intended "as well for us as for the King; for we lay the most part of all last week in that same lodging"; and she believed she would herself have fallen victim "if God in His mercy had not preserved us." It really did not seem worth while to blow up a house with gunpowder for the sake of killing one unprotected man whom almost everybody wanted to be rid of! And there is no reason why Mary should have wished to deceive Beaton, as he was her own confidential minister and had recently written warning her to double her guards, as he had heard from the Spanish ambassador of a "formidable enterprise" on foot for her destruction. It is to the credit of Mary's honesty that neither to Beaton nor at home did she assume a grief she could not humanly feel. Horror for Darnley's murder did overwhelm her — although she was far from foreseeing how inescapably it was to lead to her own downfall — and she assured Beaton of her determination to avenge the crime. But after the poor traitorous youth had been given Christian burial and consigned to the royal vault at Holyrood, she made no pretense at a lengthy court mourning. In fact, her nerves were so shattered that a few days after the funeral — but not before a reward of two thousand pounds had been offered by her Privy Council for the apprehension of the murderers — she was ordered by her physician to Seaton on the Firth of Forth. About a hundred members of the court went with her, while the infant heir was left for safe-keeping with the dependable Earl and Countess of Mar.

Meanwhile strange and ominous things were happening

in bloody Edinburgh. Placards began appearing in the streets — whether inspired by the Maitland group or by the instinct of the populace nobody knows — directly accusing Bothwell of the crime, even displaying his picture with the legend "This is the murderer of the King." As usual, the defiant Earl fell back upon his primitive ideals, declaring that "if he knew who were the setters up of the bills and writings he would wash his hands in their blood." Significantly enough, Moray — who had returned to town after the Darnley murder and was not yet off upon his somewhat suspicious visit to London and the Continent — dined confidentially with Bothwell during this interval. And, as so often happens in times of hysterical tenseness, a madman ran through the town declaring that he himself had "shed innocent blood" and demanding justice upon those who had inspired him.

Far more potent demands for public vengeance were pouring in upon the distraught Queen: demands from her father-in-law the Earl of Lennox, even from Elizabeth and Catherine de Medici. So finally the Privy Council decreed that James Hepburn, Earl of Bothwell, should be tried before his peers on April 12th. As the day approached some four thousand of his Border followers, fully armed, rode into Edinburgh on their shaggy ponies, and when the hour came he himself proceeded to the Tolbooth for trial in state upon his own horse. Both Lennox — who seems rather understandably to have been afraid to bring his charges personally before the court — and a somewhat superfluous messenger from Elizabeth, pleaded ineffectually for a delay. The Earl of Argyle, who presided at the assize, saw no reason to defer the proceedings: and his jury promptly brought in a verdict acquitting Bothwell of all "art and part of the said slaughter of the King." Sitting on this jury were many of the leading lords of Scotland, boasting such names as Roth, Cassillis, Caithness, Ross, Hamilton, Gordon of Lochinvar, Ogilvy, Cockburn of Langton, Herries, and Mowbray.

Nonetheless, the doom of Henry Darnley was to mean the doom of Mary Stuart, also.

CHAPTER XVI

THE REIGN OF BOTHWELL

IMMEDIATELY after Bothwell's trial there was a meeting of the Scottish Estates in Edinburgh. It was a very conciliatory Parliament, trying to please everybody — except, of course, the always feared Catholic minority. It granted extra favors and support to the Kirk; restored most of Huntley's forfeited birthright; extended new lands to Moray, Maitland, and Morton; and confirmed Bothwell in his captaincy of Dunbar Castle. This indomitable and incorrigible Earl of Bothwell, James Hepburn, was, in fact, the self-appointed hero of the hour. It was he who carried the scepter before the anxious Queen at the closing of Parliament: and as yet few seemed to realize his determination to possess both Queen and scepter.

The man was a typical product of his background — a "child of tumult" whose life had known little but violence. His father Patrick Hepburn, the fourth Earl of Bothwell, was an early convert to Protestantism and seems to have been divorced from his wife before James was ten years old. In spite of this he was one of Marie de Guise's most loyal supporters. The boy, oddly enough, received more than the usual education of the day from his Catholic uncle, the Bishop of Moray; and later on he must also have absorbed some of the superficial graces of Marie's Frenchified court.

He also absorbed so abiding an abhorrence of England that he proved contemptuous of English bribes or favors. His sense of duty in public matters was rather strong, but he seems to have had no personal morality. Religion was evidently quite unreal to him, his professed Protestantism being little more than a superstitious and Knoxian antipathy to Rome. What he believed in, increasingly as time went on, was *himself* and his right to take from the world what he wanted. And if this egotism made him one of the most efficient officers of the crown, it also encouraged him in the idea that the crown might well be his.

By the time of Darnley's murder, Bothwell's high-handed ways had made him so universally feared or hated that it is impossible to get any unbiased opinion of him. But it is interesting to read the comment of Throckmorton after one of his early visits to France. What the usually discerning English ambassador said of James Hepburn was that he was a "glorious, rash and hazardous young man," and that "his adversaries should have an eye to him." When the red-headed, strong-chinned Earl came so vitally and helpfully into Mary's life — at the time of Moray's rebellion and again after Rizzio's murder — he was in his early thirties, but certainly no less rash and probably no less glorious. He was one of the few protectors to whom she could turn. And he exerted over her the fascination always held by the aggressive and elemental man for the confused and overcivilized woman.

The quality of Bothwell's own feeling for Mary must remain an open question, since love seems to have been for him chiefly a mingling of desire and the will to conquer — with a certain masculine protectiveness and possessiveness thrown in. On both sides there was an infatuation understandable enough under the circumstances; and among these circumstances must be remembered the highly irregular conditions of his marriage to Lady Jean Gordon. This daughter of the Catholic Huntleys had, like her brother Lord George, early lapsed into Protestantism. It was in the Protestant kirk that she was married to Bothwell in the February of 1566; so that the dispensation from consanguinity, which her mother, Lady Huntley, had insisted upon securing, was never used. As a matter of fact, their union was probably not even legal, as Bothwell had never been divorced from the Danish wife he had secretly married and abandoned some years before. But however questionable his marital status may have seemed to Mary, she was still faced by his involvement in the Darnley murder. She knew that the Scotch acquittal would weigh very lightly against the threatening judgments of England, France, Spain, and Rome. And she was not yet mad enough to forget the queenly honor of which she was jealous even upon the scaffold, nor the doubly royal inheritance she was determined to pass on to her son. Her one hope — and she had always a blind and pathetic power of hoping — lay in the decency of delay.

For such scruples Bothwell had, of course, neither understanding nor respect. He had now no doubt that Mary was succumbing, if she had not already succumbed, to the imperious passion of his wooing — as had every other woman whom he tried to conquer, with the single exception of his wife Lady Jean! — so he determined to act. It was exactly one week after his legal whitewashing that he gave his famous or infamous supper at Ainsley's Tavern in Edinburgh. To this were invited all the lords already in town for the close of Parliament, and most of them thought best to attend. There was much good food, more and even better drink: and as a dramatic finale the host rose up to read aloud the inevitable bond he had drawn up ready for their signatures. Like most bonds of the time it began innocently

enough with the statement that, although the Earl of Bothwell had been tried and acquitted of the murder of the
Queen's late husband, and had offered to prove his innocence by the law of arms (single combat), he was still
"calumniated by various persons"; wherefore his brother
lords and all their kin promised to "maintain his quarrel
with their bodies, goods and gear." Then came the thunder-
bolt — the proposal that "as her Majesty is now destitute of
husband, in which solitary sort the Commonweal cannot
permit her Highness to continue, if it should please her so
far to humble herself by taking one of her own born subjects
and marry the said Earl, they will maintain and fortify him
against all that would hinder or disturb the said marriage as
common enemies, and therein bestow their lives and goods
as they should answer to God and on their honor and
fidelity."

It was one of the breathless moments of history. If any
of the Scottish lords had dared to outface Bothwell, refusing
or even questioning his demand for the Queen, she might
yet have been saved. But no one did dare — not even her
Lord Chancellor, the Earl of Morton, who had probably
known in advance what was brewing and knew also how it
could be turned to his own triumph. After he had signed,
along with Argyle, who had presided at Bothwell's trial, and
Huntley, the complacent brother-in-law who followed him
about like a dog, the others could not refuse. Maitland of
Lethington had seen to it that he was not present and Moray
had seen to it that he was out of the country. Why should
the others bother about their honor and fidelity and answering to God? If the scrap of paper proved troublesome
they had always the weapon of civil war.

The Queen is said to have been both angry and indignant
when she heard of Bothwell's imperious act, and she had
every cause to be. He had, to overcome her hesitancy, fallen

back upon the only argument he himself understood; not
realizing that his thinly veiled duress might strengthen the
opposition of a woman so conscious of her queenhood. Sir
James Melville, whose *Memoirs* are generally reliable in
spite of his antagonism to Mary's religion, tells of a visit of
the brave Lord Herries who, having had no part in the
Ainsley Tavern pact, came to Edinburgh to convince the
Queen that many of her subjects feared a marriage with
Bothwell would endanger her own "honor and dignity and
the safety of the prince" her son. She assured him "there
was no such thing in her mind." A few days later Melville
himself brought to Mary a letter he had received from a
Scottish agent in London, protesting that by such a marriage
she would "lose the favor of God, her own reputation, and
the hearts of all England, Ireland and Scotland." She read
the missive in grieved silence, and passed it on to Maitland
who somewhat cynically advised Melville to get away from
court before Bothwell's return.

So there was a temporary coolness between Mary Stuart
and her importunate lover when, on April 21st, she set out
with Maitland, Melville, young Huntley, and others to visit
the royal infant at Stirling Castle. She spent two days there
and finding the child's care satisfactory rested overnight at
Linlithgow, for she was still unwell — starting back to Edinburgh on a date which must have been both precious and
nostalgic: that 24th of April which marked the anniversary
of her marriage to the gentle Dauphin, François. It would be
likely that her distraught mind had floated far away in
memories as she cantered on. If so she was brutally wakened
up when, a few miles outside of Edinburgh, she heard the
sound of hooves and suddenly found her small escort surrounded by "a great company" of armed horsemen. They
were Bothwell's men; and Bothwell rode forward to command the Queen and her outnumbered companions to

follow him back to Dunbar Castle. There was no time for thought or parley. Here was the old story of the Scottish sovereign abducted by the robber baron: only this time the sovereign was a woman, and the baron the man she both loved and feared. A few of her followers were allowed to go on to Edinburgh, and to these Mary whispered a plea that they "charge the towne to be in armour for her rescue." Then she rode on to her rendezvous with destiny. Maitland and Melville rode with her; and the latter tells of hearing Bothwell boast that he would marry the Queen "who would or who would not — yea, whether she would herself or not."

There is no more controversial episode in all Mary's controversial story than this preposterous kidnaping. That its details had been carefully engineered by Lord George Huntley under Bothwell's orders there seems no doubt. The idea that it was engineered with the Queen's knowledge and collusion, as gossipy historians were quick to charge, has no proof or even plausibility. If Mary Stuart had been ready or willing to wed her pursuer, she had but to cite the bond signed by her lords as excuse. Practically alone she was holding out against them and against him. What she probably hoped was that, later on, when the problems of Darnley's questionable murder and Bothwell's questionable nuptials were cleared up, there might be a State marriage performed with the rites of her Church and for the professed good of the kingdom. And clearly any such dream — or any other dream of a foreign alliance later on — would be wrecked by the abject outcome of this abduction and seduction. For twelve days Bothwell held her prisoner in Dunbar castle, and Bothwell was no respecter of man or woman. Melville did not hesitate to report to her lords that the Queen had been ravished: to which Maitland added that he himself would have been slain by the ruthless Earl had not Mary stood between them. But before resorting to force,

James Hepburn had urged his devotion and his ability to keep peace in Scotland, and — more persuasively still! — had confided to her the story of his wandering, unhappy, and adventurous life. When they rode back to Edinburgh on May 6th his reign had already begun. He himself walked beside her horse's head, "leading the Queen's Majesty by the bridle as captive" — and he had arranged that the cannon of the Castle should thunder out "most magnificently" in welcome. Mary had not even the right to be called Bothwell's mistress, he was so obviously her master: but she had consented to become as soon as possible his legal wife. Apparently most of the Scottish lords agreed with Melville that "the Queen could not but marry him. . . ."

Already, in fact, the machinery of divorce had been set in motion. Lady Jean, who apparently preferred Bothwell as lover and King of Scotland rather than as husband, appealed to the Protestant Court for a dissolution of their marriage on the grounds of his adultery with a servant. And to insure the success of his own appeal for a Catholic declaration of nullity, she even hid away that unused dispensation secured by her mother because she and Hepburn were related in the fourth degree. It was all a tragic and scandalous farce; and while these measures were proceeding Bothwell is said to have continued to visit Jean on terms of amorous intimacy. It is not unlikely that her breezy indifference did serve as a spur to his passion, while the Queen's heartbroken submission already inspired only satiety and resentment.

From this time until Mary's incarceration in England the whole tangled story is further complicated by the hectic and usually hostile gossip of the times: some of which is worth repeating simply because it colored the judgment of her contemporaries and has colored the judgment of the centuries, too. For instance, there is Kirkaldy of Grange's reckless tale that *somebody* had heard the Queen say of Bothwell that she "cares not to lose France, England and her own country for him, and will go with him to the world's end in a white petticoat ere she leaves him." It does not sound in the least like Mary Stuart, who always spoke with great discretion even when she acted rashly. But if for awhile both spirit and body were under the man's sway, she was soon enough disillusioned. His jealousy both of her power and her person was soon as exigent as Darnley's own. And being a strong tyrant instead of a weak one, he found far more effective ways of wrecking her peace and alienating the Scottish lords; although, as she confessed pathetically in one of her letters, his words could at times be gentle enough in spite of his rough acts! When Master John Craig, the preacher in charge of St. Giles during Knox's absence, protested against calling the banns for this royal marriage, Bothwell threatened to have him hanged. And on the day before this calamitous ceremony there was a bitter scene between bride and groom: both Melville and the gentle French ambassador Du Croc hearing the Queen threaten suicide, and beg Arthur Erskine to bring a dagger that she might take her life. Mary Stuart was as close to despair at this time as she was ever to come, which is saying much. And no doubt this remorse grew partly from her realization that by yielding to Bothwell she had betrayed the trust of those to whom she stood as a symbol of the Old Faith in Scotland and the North. As a final humiliation he insisted upon having the mock marriage performed by his kinsman Adam Bothwell, the apostate and political Bishop of Orkney, and "according to the Protestant form." It took place in the great hall of Holyrood House — not in the chapel — in the dark early morning of May 15th, 1567; and as there was no celebration afterward, we are not told whether Mary bothered to change her mourning or not. Huntley, the ex-brother-in-law, was present and a handful of the Bothwell henchmen; but Morton, Maitland, and the other lords were absent and biding their time. A few days later Sir William Drury wrote from Berwick to Lord Cecil that he heard from those who had visited her "that the Queen is the most changed woman of face that in so little time, without extremity of sickness, they have seen."

There is a very human paradox in the letter which Mary dispatched by the Bishop of Dunblane to young King Charles IX, to "the Queen, our very good Mother," and to the Cardinal of Lorraine, attempting to explain her marriage to Bothwell. She does not deny his use of force, admitting that the Earl — whom she had now raised to the Dukedom of Orkney — had "used us otherwise than we would have wished." But she cites his many patriotic services to Marie de Guise and herself, and finally begs them to accept the inevitable; to "make the best of it," as she herself must, and receive him honorably as her husband. She adds that in her quandary she had neither support nor advice from any man in Scotland; and that although she had no time to consult the Papal authorities about the conditions of her marriage (as, of course, she should have done), she would never give up her religion for "any man on earth." A similar but less intimate letter was sent to Elizabeth by Melville, in which Mary stressed her inability to keep peace between the rival Scottish factions, and all too optimistically assured her sister Queen of the Earl's acquittal of the murder charges and the complete legality of her marriage: both matters which, one might have thought, Anne Boleyn's daughter was scarcely in a position to question!

Underneath this natural attempt to save face, the Queen's position was increasingly perilous. Reports are constant that Bothwell soon sought possession of the young Prince and that his "disdainful" treatment left Mary scarcely a day in peace or without tears. Her spiritual desolation must have been extreme. It is true that she had sown the bitter winds; that pushed half by love and half by desperation she had accepted the conditions of this mad marriage instead of fighting them. But it is not less tragic that, after the scandalous union, even the Dominican who had acted as her confessor left her and returned to France. Quite possibly the Earl himself was responsible for this departure, as he was jealous of all Catholic influence and had no use for any but the most venal churchmen. At any rate the priest later testified that until the crisis of the Bothwell affair he had never seen "a woman of greater virtue, courage and uprightness" than Mary Stuart. What the repercussions were in Rome one gathers from a letter sent by the statesman, Cardinal Alessandroni, reporting of Pope Pius V: "With regard to the Queen of Scots, it is not his intention to have any further communication with her, unless indeed in time to come he shall see some better sign of her life and religion."

So, alone in her misery, Mary was left standing outside St. Peter's gate. But the gate was at least left ajar. And a sentence from that Father Hay who had accompanied De Gouda on his fruitless visit five years before is prophetic in its charity. "It may be," he writes to his Jesuit superiors, "that someday all things will cooperate for the good of that sinful woman, and that she will become the doer of great deeds who formerly would not consent to sound counsel."

Then he begs for Mary Stuart the prayers of the Society. God alone could have known how desperately she was to need them.

CHAPTER XVII

THE WHIRLWIND OF CARBERRY HILL

Scarcely two weeks after the marriage of Mary and Bothwell, Lord Herries tells us a council was formed by the Scottish lords "to seek the liberty of the Queen, to preserve the life of the Prince, and to pursue them that murdered the King." These motives were, of course, far from ingenuous: but at face value they offered a rallying ground of apparent justice where both the Catholic and Protestant nobles might meet. Probably few except the masterminds of the triumvirate realized that here was the germ of a far more serious rebellion than the one-sided affair engineered by Moray after the Darnley marriage. For the fear of Bothwell — now flaunting his new title of Duke of Orkney and the Shetlands — was more universal and better founded than the early jealousy and resentment against the "long lad" from England. If the superb James Hepburn succeeded in attaining even the crown matrimonial — as he would undoubtedly — he would be King of Scotland indeed: so much King that the Queen would be overshadowed. Sir James Melville records, too, the general impression that Bothwell was "very earnest to get the young Prince in his hands." What he does not add, but what history was to prove, was that many other lords were equally earnest in this same cause, wishing to hold the helpless heir hostage for their own dominance of Scotland. Mary's greatest peril lay now in the fact that she had given her country what it wanted most — a King who could not rule. She was no longer expendable.

There is no way of learning how much of this danger she herself understood: probably only the most obvious points, and assuredly not the major plot being hatched for her abdication. She made no effort as yet to give Bothwell the crown matrimonial which Darnley had abused, nor to withdraw her "dearest son" from the care of the Earl of Mar. But she evidently had no conception how quickly matters were moving and had not yet perspective enough to seek, as she wished later on at Lochleven, "little by little to draw home again unto her obedience the whole body of her subjects." The woman, yielding to the violence of circumstance, had bartered her world for love. It was but human that she should try to hide even from herself the fact that her love was not worth the price — and that poor as it was, she was already losing it.

With civil war almost at the door of Holyrood House, Mary withdrew with her lord to Borthwick Castle, within nearer reach of his Border troops. Already she had seen the subtle Maitland slip away from her attenuated court "without leavetaking," to join the disaffected lords. Already, in urgent need of money, she had directed much of her plate — including the golden font sent by Queen Elizabeth for the christening of the infant James — to be melted and minted into currency. Already she and Bothwell had issued a proclamation calling upon all loyal "noblemen, knights, esquires, gentlemen and yeomen" of Scotland to meet them at Muirhead Abbey on June 12th, "with six day's victuals, and every man to come in warlike manner."

The faithful levies had assembled willingly enough when

she called upon them after the Darnley marriage, but this time the response was slow and niggardly. And on June 10th the powerful Lord Hume — who incidentally, had not hesitated to sign the Ainsley Tavern bond — surrounded Borthwick with a company of cavalrymen demanding the surrender of Bothwell. The latter, never an easy prey to catch, had already escaped and was riding fast toward Dunbar. So the revolting Lords of the Congregation contented themselves with inviting the Queen to join their pursuit of her husband; and upon her refusal, with berating her Majesty in language "too evil and unseemly to be told." Wearying finally of this sport and lacking as yet a determined leader, they rode back toward Edinburgh for further instructions. Meanwhile Mary, realizing the desperate necessity for quick action, slipped into page's clothing, donned spurred boots, and galloped off apparently quite alone to join Bothwell. He met her en route; and together the man and woman whose union had spelled ruin from the first rode on through the night to his memory-haunted fortress of Dunbar.

Destiny had set June 15th, exactly one month after their wedding day, for the final scene of this tragic romance. The Queen rode out of the castle gates clothed in the only woman's garb she could borrow at Dunbar — a scarlet petticoat, peasant waist, muffler, and hat of black velvet. But by her side floated the royal pennant of Scotland with its Stuart lion rampant, and before long Bothwell was commanding more than three thousand troops. Looking down from Carberry Hill, not many miles from Edinburgh, she saw at the far side of a little brook the larger and far better equipped army of the rebels, commanded by the Earl of Morton and Kirkaldy of Grange. Bloodshed was always painful to her, and she may have felt intuitively that it would be futile, too. So she commissioned good Monsieur du Croc, the French ambassador who had apparently joined her, to seek some means of making peace with the revolting lords. He found them full of defiance and scornful of her offer of pardon for their treason; although Morton sent back the hypocritical message that they were in arms not against the Queen but against the Duke of Orkney, murderer of her late husband, and that if her Majesty "would remove him from her company" they would yield her obedience. Bothwell's reply to this had something of his old glory and rashness. His voice was as defiant as their own as he rode forward declaring that fortune was a prize to be won by those who chose and dared, and offering to prove his innocence by single combat with any knight of equal rank. Mary frowned upon this heroic but somewhat outworn gesture; and in any case, before a suitable champion could be found on the revolting side, it was too late. The insurgent forces were already crossing the brook to begin attack; while Mary's small army, failing to get expected re-enforcements, began disappearing into the hills or fraternizing with the enemy.

Faced then with almost certain defeat, Mary once again sent a messenger armed with a white flag, asking Kirkaldy of Grange to offer terms of surrender. He came himself; and as he knelt courteously enough before her Majesty, Melville reports that Bothwell gave orders for his shooting — which was only prevented by Mary's appeal to honor. This particular piece of dastardry probably never happened, for other participants say that the insurgent leader brought a private paper advising Bothwell that his enemies were quite willing for him to escape. In any case the terms were the same as before: if the Queen parted from her problematical husband the lords would return to her allegiance.

A few hurried words passed between the two whose love had been as heavy with doom as that of Tristram and Iseult. Then Mary Stuart looked into the eyes of James Hepburn

for the last time. With a handful of followers he galloped
off toward Dunbar and the seacoast, escaping eventually to
Denmark. She, in a daze of pain and accompanied only by
the faithful Mary Seaton and Mary Livingston, permitted
Kirkaldy to lead "her horse by the bridle down the hill to
the waiting lords" — while "all her company scattered and
rode their way" into the night.

Kirkaldy had scarcely been Mary's friend, although he
was to return later to her allegiance, but perhaps he did
not realize into what a traitors' trap he led his Queen. She
herself realized at long last: and her fighting Stuart blood
rose in a fury of words as she saw half-veiled triumph and
defiance upon the faces of Morton and Maitland and heard
an undertone of vituperation from other Lords of the Congregation. She had been tricked into surrender, and it was
not as queen but as captive that she was surrounded by her
enemies and compelled to ride back to Edinburgh preceded
by one of those insulting banners in which Scotland seems
to have specialized. Hypocritically enough but also significantly enough, considering the men who bore it, this showed
her infant heir kneeling beside Darnley's naked corpse with
outstretched hands, and bore the legend: *"Judge and defend
my cause, O Lord."* As they came into the capital its streets
were thick with howling and milling mobs, already worked
up into fury by the propaganda of preacher and politician.
Almost fainting now from exhaustion and hunger, Mary
heard raucous cries of "Burn the whore — burn the murderer
of her husband!" The waves of hate, so long diked-up and
deflected, were breaking at last at her feet. Half-submerged,
she still fought back her tears, calling down upon her de-
tractors the just wrath of Heaven and earth.

Clothed in the battered, bourgeoise raiment borrowed at
Dunbar, the Queen of Scotland and Dowager of France was
carried, helpless and hysterical, not into her palace of Holy-

rood but into the house of the Provost of Edinburgh on High Street. Even her two devoted handmaidens were forbidden to follow. She was too distraught to touch any food, although she had tasted none all day: one hopes too distraught to hear any longer the din of the half-drunk populace outside as she lay stretched upon the hard cot. One more rumor handed down by Melville says that in this nadir hour Mary found means to write briefly to her "Dear Heart," Bothwell, begging him to believe that their separation was only temporary — and that the letter was promptly conveyed by a servant not to him but to the rebel lords, whom it still further incensed. All this is not too likely, and the paper has never been produced. But it may be she did make this final attempt to signal the lover who had so often saved her, and did suffer the final bitterness of finding her signal unanswered. At any rate the Lords of the Congregation needed no egging on. It was no part of their game to pursue Bothwell, who knew too many of their own guilty secrets. But the superfluous Queen was in their power and they were determined to keep her there: by force and also by defamation.

By morning Mary was on the verge of delirium. There is a heartbreaking story of her opening the window of her solitary chamber and leaning out, her auburn hair hanging loose and her blouse torn and dishevelled — only to be faced by the nightmare banner and the other nightmare of the still jeering rabble. But looking closely, her bloodshot eyes discerned a tall, familiar figure trying to hasten by unnoticed. It was Maitland of Lethington, her Secretary of State: and to him she called so piercingly that he was compelled to enter and seek the cell where she had been locked alone. Bitter words passed between them: Mary's accusations of his part in the Darnley murder and her own betrayal, his own denunciation of Bothwell. . . . But the statesman had begun to fear both the fury and the fickleness of mob psychology. He knew that already one of Bothwell's followers, the Laird of Blackadder, had been captured and executed without trial, "solemnly calling God to witness his innocence." And he knew also that the decent craftsmen of Edinburgh had protested to the Provost against their Queen's arrest, threatening to unfurl the Blue Blanket which was their symbol of a royal emergency, and to rally their members to her rescue. So toward evening he and Morton decided that the wretched woman might safely be transferred to Holyrood House, accompanied by a band of soldiers still carrying the abusive banner.

When darkness fell upon the city, its Queen was forced to mount her horse again and start for the first of her many prisons, with two sinister guards whom she had once pardoned for treason: young Ruthven, son of the protagonist at Rizzio's assassination, and that brutal Earl of Lindsay who was henchman and brother-in-law of Moray. From Leith they took ship for Burntisland, and as dawn was breaking reached the island-castle of Lochleven. Mary, who had not known their destination, was probably beyond sensing how ominous and eloquent was this choice — the home of Moray's mother Lady Douglas and her son Sir William. Nor could she know that within good reach across Border and Channel, the Earl of Moray, Lord James Stuart himself, waited discreetly for the next play, when he should be recalled — drafted, as politicians now describe it — as Regent of Scotland.

CHAPTER XVIII

LOCHLEVEN INTERLUDE

$\mathbf{A}$T LOCHLEVEN, in the hands of her father's
quondam mistress — that Margaret Erskine who had become the wife and now the widow of Lord Robert Douglas
— Mary Stuart suffered the most complete nervous collapse
since her almost fatal attack at Jedburgh. She remained
"fifteen days or more without eating, drinking or conversing
with the inmates of the house, so that many thought she
would have died." Her French apothecary was sent for; and
she seems to have been nursed rather gently by one Jane
Kennedy, by Lady Douglas herself and a young French maid
named Marie Courcelles. It is a good commentary that Mary
was always loved and served so faithfully by women — unless,
like Catherine de Medici, Elizabeth, and a few others, they
happened to be jealous of her personal or political power.

Outside the sickroom door stood sentinels, and both
Ruthven and Lindsay remained a few weeks at the castle.
But they did not attempt to enter the Queen's chamber
until, early in July, they came accompanied by her former
envoy to England, Master Robert Melville, brother of the
more celebrated Sir James. It was clear they all wished to
discuss something momentous, but Mary was too weak to
listen and they were obliged to leave without broaching it.
A week or so later Melville returned alone, and this time

he admitted that what the confederate lords desired was
their Queen's formal abdication in favor of the baby James,
and letters appointing a Regent. She can scarcely have been
surprised, but was not yet ready to give her answer. Upon
his third visit he evidently suggested an annulment of the
Bothwell marriage, for Mary gave as one reason for her
reluctance the belief that she was pregnant, and unwilling
to impugn her child's legitimacy. Then, returning to the
matter of the abdication, Robert Melville offered a surprising solution: he pointed out — and even produced a
letter of Throckmorton's giving the same advice from Elizabeth! — that if Mary signed any such paper under duress
she would be entirely free to repudiate it when liberated.
This was perfectly good legal and even canonical advice, but
Mary still hesitated to sign away the kingdom for which she
had already suffered so much. Or perhaps in some secret
way she knew that back on June 29th a bond attacking her
imprisonment and swearing "to make our exact diligence
to put her at liberty" had been signed by the Archbishop
of St. Andrews and the lords of Huntley, Argyle, Herries,
Fleming, and others, while the whole Hamilton clan was
already gathering against the new regime.

Her signature was finally gained by those brutal methods
with which she was to become all too familiar in the years
ahead. Ruthven and Lindsay appeared at her door with two
notaries, and ordering her women from the room practically commanded their Queen, under threat of murder,
to sign the two papers they brought. These were then read
aloud to her: the first an abdication of the throne in favor
of her son, the other an appointment of her bastard brother
Moray as Regent. With dignity Mary Stuart took the quill
and signed. Then, with her unquenchable candor, she protested that she would repudiate these forced signatures at
her first opportunity of freedom. Lindsay replied that he and

her other jailors would be careful that no such opportunity occurred. Then her tormentors left. A few days later, on July 27th, the sick woman was startled to hear the cannon of Lochleven booming and to see the reflection of bonfires about its lake. A sentinel gave the information that they were celebrating the coronation of the new King, James VI. His mother closed her eyes and lay silent. She must have been thinking of all the tragic story that had come to life since the birth of that son a little over a year before.

Early in August the prisoner learned that her brother, the Earl of Moray, had returned to Edinburgh; and she immediately and it seems even hopefully began sending letters begging him to come to her. By the middle of the month he condescended to visit Lochleven, accompanied by the Earls of Morton and Atholl. The dethroned Queen insisted upon seeing him alone, and evidently used every persuasion in her power to win back the friendship and support which even yet she could not believe lost forever. Nothing came of the interview, of course — except her final realization of her brother's complete treachery. When she pleaded for her liberty he replied with his usual cold evasion that "It lay not in his power, nor was it good for her to seek it nor presently to have it, in many respects." The embittered brother was master now; already her son and her possessions were in his power. One week later he was officially installed as Regent of Scotland — swearing to persecute all enemies of the "true kirk of God," and even recalling John Knox, whom he had formerly found too extreme. For awhile it seemed that the Lords of the Congregation had their ideal ruler: but Melville's journal records not only his harshness toward Mary but also the growing arrogance and love of flattery by which he lost even his closest supporters. Before him lay less than three years of troubled triumph, while he sank ever deeper in treason and duplicity. Then the hate he had so carefully fanned was to turn back against himself and Scotland was to see one more assassination.

For Mary Stuart it was a winter of misery which, because of the "iron curtain" of her captors, remains largely a winter of mystery, too. That she was dangerously ill is admitted by all sides. Some report that she suffered a miscarriage of Bothwell's child during those dark Lochleven days. Others, including Prince Labanoff, accept the story handed down by the French ambassador, Castelnau de la Mauvissière, which tells of the Queen bearing a daughter during the dark February of 1568: and that the baby was secretly transported to France, where she eventually died as a nun at Soissons. There is drama and romance and a certain poetic justice in the thought of a child of that fatal union — which so cruelly hurt the cause of Catholicism in Scotland — consecrating her life to prayer and expiation. It is the sort of thing which ought to happen and sometimes does in life. Unfortunately no documents have so far been found to verify it.

In any case, by spring the stricken Queen of Scotland had recovered health and spirit sufficiently to begin brooding upon plans to escape from her prison. It is rumored that Lady Douglas — in spite of a natural fear of angering her son Moray — secretly favored such an enterprise: it is certain that her younger son, Sir George Douglas, had fallen completely under the sway of Mary. So, too, had the anomalous but highly ingenious youth known about the castle as Little Willie, and suspected of being a natural son of its owner, Sir William Douglas. These kinsmen threw themselves with a romantic enthusiasm which Mary was never to forget into schemes for her freedom, and in March one of them very nearly succeeded. Then it was that the Queen, in peasant dress and with a muffler about her face, slipped out of the castle with the laundresses who came regularly to collect

its soiled linen. She herself carried a fardel or bundle, and
arrived safely at the lake's edge with the group. But the
dainty smallness of her feet as she climbed into the boat,
and later of her hands as she tried to adjust the scarf more
tightly, betrayed her to the oarsmen. They rowed the exile
promptly back to Lochleven. And this time the disconsolate
Willie was expelled by his alarmed father — or whatever
relation Sir William was. Sir George had already been
banished from his home on the advice of Moray — who
seems to have felt the youth was on the Queen's side, although he could have had no suspicion of the extent of his
allegiance. But both young men took their exile in the usual
Scottish manner. Little Willie soon smuggled himself back
and was reinstated as cupbearer to Sir William; while
George installed himself in the woods just across the lake,
where he was in frequent touch with John Beaton — brother
of the Archbishop who remained Mary's French ambassador
— and with the various loyal lords who were gathering to
force her freedom. And by this time Marie Courcelles was
so thoroughly won over to the Queen's cause that she could
be trusted to convey letters across the lake at any time.

One of these letters went to Catherine de Medici at the
end of March, and another to Archbishop Beaton ("Monsieur de Glasgow"), both begging the support of France and
warning secrecy: since "should it be known that I have
written, it may cost a great many lives, put my own in peril
and cause me to be still more closely guarded." On the first
of May an even more interesting epistle was written by
Mary to her cousin Elizabeth. In it she tells of her "weary
imprisonment and the wrongs I have received from those
on whom I have conferred so many benefits," and suggests
to Elizabeth the danger of this example to other sovereigns.
Then she reminds her of a ring once sent her by the
English Queen, with the promise that on receiving it back

she would assist her Scottish sister "in any time of trouble."
Recounting rather ingenuously that she cannot send the
ring, since Moray has seized all her belongings, she begs
her to listen to the bearer of this letter — probably Beaton
— as to her own self. The close of the letter is, in the light
of future events, significant: "God keep you from misfortunes, and grant me patience and His grace that I may one
day recount my calamities to yourself, when I will tell you
more than I dare to write, which may prove of no small
service to yourself."

The next day Mary Stuart escaped from her prison at
Lochleven. How this was contrived in the evening of May
2nd, when Sir William was so drowsy over his cups that
Willie Douglas was able to purloin the key of the castle's
outer gate from before his very eyes, is a fascinating and
intricate story. The time had been carefully chosen. The chief
boatman was laid up after an accident, and Mary had arranged to have the chief sentry off in Edinburgh cashing
one of her own drafts. Whether Lady Douglas, coerced into
active compassion for this daughter of her girlhood's royal
lover, saw to it that the grounds were deserted is open to
suspicion. In any case, the Queen, wrapped in a dark cloak,
slipped easily through the courtyard with Jane Kennedy and
Marie Courcelles, and — joining little Willie — through the
castle gate. After that it was but a few moments' work to
cross the grounds leading to the lake and leap into one of
the lightly tethered boats. With Willie bending over the
oars they were soon far out from shore, and in the moonlight
Mary rose up to wave the signal of her white veil. On the
opposite bank the devoted old friend John Beaton and the
adoring new one George Douglas were ready to welcome
their Queen, and to lift her and her two companions upon
the waiting ponies.

As they galloped desperately toward the Firth of Forth

they were joined by Lord Seaton with half a hundred horsemen; and as many more — led by Lord Claude Hamilton, the younger and loyally Catholic son of Châtelheraut — met them when they had forded the waters. Together then all hurried through the night to Seaton's Niddry Castle in West Lothian, where men and horses and the hard-spent Queen were allowed a few hours' rest.

Early in the morning Lord Herries — who, a year before, had given his consent to the Queen's banishment but was now returned to his allegiance and would not again falter — rode up to Niddry with his followers. About noon the company, now some two hundred strong, set out for Hamilton Palace, where there was to be a gathering of the clans and a conference of the loyal lords. For the first time in many months Mary breathed in the thrill of freedom — and heard the thrill of cheering — as she rode on.

CHAPTER   XIX

THE LAST STAND: LANGSIDE —
AND ENGLAND

It would seem that Mary's own wish was to
retire for awhile to Dumbarton Castle, "where everyone
could have free access to her," and so gradually win back
the allegiance of her kingdom — in spite of Moray or Maitland or Morton. Probably she could not yet have succeeded;
for this evil trinity, like all men who hold power, held
patronage also. And there is considerable truth in Melville's
belief that the whole desperate venture of her escape came
a little too soon: "ere the time was ripe enough to recover
the hearts of the subjects, who were yet alienated" by calumny and suspicion. At any rate she was, as usual, overruled by
her lords — particularly the Hamiltons — who feared she
might again be captured, and believed their best hope lay
in open battle.

So there was the usual call to arms of all loyal Scotchmen:
and a rather unusual manifesto, telling off the rebels with
true Scotch vituperation as "crafty, perjured foxes," "heirs
to Judas, sons of Satan and of the progeny of cruel Cain."
Before long such eminent earls as Argyle, Eglinton, Cassillis,
Livingston, Fleming, and Roth had joined the standard of
the dethroned Queen. There were many of Bothwell's hardy
Border troops, and some Highlanders, although Huntley had

not yet arrived from the north with his promised army. From Bothwell himself there was, of course, no word. But in justice to the man who seems to have been looking after himself rather than after the woman whose life he had pulled down into ruin, it should be added that about this time the fugitive Duke was probably offering his islands of Orkney and Shetland to the Danish King, in a vain hope of rallying him to Mary Stuart's cause. Instead, it appears that Bothwell himself was detained in a kind of protective custody in Denmark for the rest of his life.

The Regent Moray's headquarters were at Glasgow this time and so only eight miles from Hamilton Castle; and knowing that Mary's troops daily increased, he wished to force an engagement before Huntley's northern re-enforcements joined them. Lord Claude Hamilton was equally impatient for battle, and seems to have been confident that the royal forces would prevail. Which army was really the larger is a matter of dispute; but there is no question at all that the insurgents, with their use of the new harquebus rather than bow and arrow, were better equipped and better organized. On May 13th, as the Queen's troops were marching quietly along the south bank of the Clyde toward Dumbarton, with Argyle in command and Herries directing the cavalry, they walked directly into a hidden nest of enemy guns near Langside, and so were compelled into immediate action. Once again Mary faced the very generals who had deceived and defeated her at Carberry Hill — Kirkaldy of Grange, Lindsay, and Morton — and once again she was hopelessly outmaneuvered. It was a brief but fateful drama which she and a few others, including her two young Douglas champions, watched from near-by Cathcart Knowe. Almost at its beginning Argyle suddenly fell senseless from his horse, which caused no little delay and confusion. Then came the old story of the bottleneck in the narrow pass, the re-enforcements which failed to arrive — and a definite if not very brilliant victory for the Regent's forces. Melville comments that there were "few slain and taken" at Langside, adding that after this defeat "Her Majesty lost all courage, which she never had done before."

But even in face of this fiasco that inextinguishable courage — this time, perhaps, the courage of desperation — soon returned. She was in mortal danger: for to be captured a second time by rebels who now had tasted victory and held the infant King in their power, would probably have meant the death they obviously desired for her. Lord Herries counseled instant flight, first to his own familiar Maxwell countryside, thence to the coast and France. Mary at first consented, but was obsessed with the idea of taking her "good cousin" Elizabeth at her word and seeking temporary shelter in England. With dogged endurance she mounted her horse and started a terrific ride of sixty miles, accompanied by Herries, the Douglas boys, and a few other faithful followers. As she wrote later to her uncle, the Cardinal, their only food was a little oatmeal and sour milk at one of the peasant cottages, and she passed the night "on the hard ground" — listening, as she never forgot, to the ominous hooting of owls. The next day they had a brief breathing space in the comparative safety of Dundrennan Abbey: but by this time Mary was adamant in her insistence upon crossing the near-by Border into England. So the heartbroken George and Willie Douglas were sent in search of a fishing boat to cross the Solway River; and on May 16th, 1568, the Queen and her companions set out upon the journey which for her, at least, was to have no return.

That evening the weary and disheveled little group landed near Workington and proceeded on foot to accept the nearby hospitality of one Sir Henry Curwen. By the next day news had perforated the English countryside; and many of the northern gentry — still loyal to their Catholic Faith — came to welcome Mary Stuart, who contrived to be gracious and regal even in the shabby black frock she had worn ever since Langside. From Workington Hall she also wrote to Elizabeth a remarkably comprehensive letter. In it she told the story of the Sctoch lords' treachery and usurpation, of her forced abdication, her escape and defeat. With great dignity she assures her sister Queen that she relies upon her help not only for personal safety but for assistance in her "just quarrel," adding frankly that she intends to solicit the same from other princes. And the long epistle ends upon this note of characteristic and winning simplicity: "I entreat you to send to fetch me as soon as you possibly can, for I am in a pitiable condition not only for a queen but for a gentlewoman; for I have nothing in the world but what I had on my person when I made my escape . . . as I hope to declare before you if it pleases you to have pity, as I trust you will . . . upon my extreme misfortune." Then praying God to give Elizabeth long life and "that consolation which I expect to receive from you," she signs herself: "Your most faithful and affectionate good sister and cousin and escaped prisoner, Marie, R."

For a little while it really looked as if Mary Stuart had made the right choice of a haven. When the deputy governor, Sir Richard Lowther, arrived to take her party on to Cockermouth, the Earl of Northumberland contested with him the honor of entertaining the royal fugitive. She was being welcomed as a Queen: and it is pleasant to remember the Cockermouth merchant who presented her with thirteen ells of red velvet, that she might also be clothed as a Queen. Within a few days Lowther evidently had instructions to install Mary at his safe but forbidding fortress of Carlisle Castle: where, with unexpected results later on, she was attended by Lady Scrope, sister of the Duke of Norfolk.

The first dissonant note was struck when Lord Scrope, warden of the Western Marches, accompanied by Sir Francis Knollys, the vice-chancellor, arrived with a direct message from Elizabeth. The Scottish Queen was so excited to hear of their approach that she bade Lord Herries to mount his horse and meet them five or six miles out of Carlisle, to give them welcome and learn their good news. But it was not good. And when Mary, hurrying into the presence chamber to greet them, read Elizabeth's curt excuse that she could not receive her personally until she was cleared of the charge of "participating" in Darnley's murder, she burst into tears of disappointment and indignation. How could she know that most of Moray's absence from Scotland had been spent in spreading this very charge in France as well as England? But her impulsive defense and assertion that "it could well be proved" how Maitland and Morton had been among the conspirators of that crime seem to have impressed the two Englishmen. They reported back to their royal mistress (who must have hated the news!) that Mary Stuart had "an eloquent tongue and a discreet head, and it seemeth by her doings she hath stout courage and a liberal heart adjoined thereto." They even warned Elizabeth to be more careful in future what messages she sent to the Queen of Scots, since "many gentlemen of divers shires" near-by had already conversed with her; hearing "her daily defenses and excuses of her innocence, with her great accusations of her enemies very eloquently told," and being strongly influenced by them. As a matter of fact, one of those who seem already to have called upon Mary and been "strongly influenced" by her was the Duke of Norfolk himself.

As for Mary, she sat down the very day of Scrope's visit and wrote to Elizabeth another letter of equal courage and dignity. In it she repeats that she had wished "above all" to come in person "to clear myself before you from those calumnious charges which they have dared to proffer against my honor": and she rightly holds the English Queen partially responsible for her present plight, since it was she who had urged pardon for the very lords who had brought it about. This letter Mary sent by the Lords Fleming and Herries, telling Elizabeth that with her consent they would proceed to France to visit her brother-in-law, Charles IX, and other good friends.

"There is nothing," she adds unanswerably, "to prevent me from applying to them but this detention, which, to speak freely to you as you do to me, I think rather harsh and strange.

How far Mary was from realizing the sinister truth of her position in England is evident from another note carried by Lord Herries. It was addressed to Elizabeth's crafty and infinitely clever Lord Treasurer, Cecil; and in it with almost incredible naïveté — or could it have been an attempt at diplomacy? — Mary asks the *benefit of his good counsel*, because of the "sincere and faithful service" he had rendered to her good sister Elizabeth and consequently to all those who are of her blood and like dignity." She even commends herself courteously to Cecil's wife and prays God to hold him "in His holy keeping!"

From this very time Cecil begins to loom across Mary's sky as a cloud of increasing doom. What the Scottish Queen's story might have been without the intervention of this truly Machiavellian minister it is impossible to guess — just as it is impossible to surmise what Elizabeth's own might have been. By his will and his wit he dominated the Queen and the official England of his day, determined to make it the greatest Protestant power in Europe: for he was violently anti-Catholic, although, as Hilaire Belloc so masterfully points out,* his hatred of the Church was rather to insure the financial and political supremacy of himself and the new nobility than because of any particular theological convictions. To him the young Catholic Mary of France and Scotland had always been a challenge — and Mary Stuart as a fugitive in England he saw as a peril and a problem of unknown possibilities. How he went about solving the problem is revealed in notes he jotted down about this time under the general head of *"Things to be considered upon the Scottish Quene coming into England."* Here we find he has already decided: "The surety of the Queen of Scots is first to be considered, that by no practice she should be conveyed out of the realm"; a little further on he is debating "Whether it be meeter that she remain on the frontier, or be brought to the middle part of England"; and, against all decent diplomatic usage, he decides to order "no English, Scottish or French to come to her without permission of her keeper, and any secret letters to be seized." Then, with consummate hypocrisy, he, whom his own people learned to call "the old fox," adds the notation: "That our ambassador signify her arrival to the French King, and that the Queen's Majesty will see her safely and honourably preserved, and will use all good means to restore her and her realm to quietness, requesting him to send no men or ships to Scotland . . . which her Majesty cannot endure." From his further notes it is evident that Cecil had determined upon some sort of a mock trial in which Moray, Maitland, and the rest of their gang were to bring accusations against Mary Stuart. These men had long been in his service and in his pay.

On June 14th one Henry Middlemore visited the captive at Carlisle with a letter in which Elizabeth again, but more courteously, excused herself from an interview on the ground

————

* *Characters of the Reformation.*

that she was already "held suspect" (she does not say by
whom!) for wishing to defend Mary against her subjects'
charges. With characteristic dissimulation she prays God
to deliver her cousin from her "evil enemies," protesting
that "there is no creature living" more desirous to hear the
proofs of her innocence than herself. "Since you put in my
hands the handling of this business," she adds, "assure
yourself I shall be so careful of your life and honour, that
yourself or any other parent could not have them more at
heart. And I promise on the word of a prince, that no
persuasion of your subjects or advice of others shall ever
induce me to move you to anything dangerous to you or
your honour."

By this time Mary had good reason to be skeptical of
"the word of a prince," and she told the messenger with her
usual directness: "If the Queen your mistress will not have
me come to her, first upon respect of getting an evil opinion,
and then as afraid to offend such princes as she sayeth do
mislike her good usage of me, I would be glad to ease her
of both fears. So I trust that if she will not give me that
help that access to her would mean and other aid as my
case requires, she will yet suffer me to go to such as will do
both the one and the other."

This reference to France and Spain must have embarrassed
Middlemore. He fenced for a few moments, then came out
with the surprise news he had kept "to make a pleasant parting." His Queen, it seems, was planning to remove Mary
closer to herself, where she might find "more pleasure and
liberty and be utterly out of danger of her enemies." The
Queen of Scots was not deceived. She demanded whether
she was to go by her own choice or as a prisoner: and getting
no satisfactory answer, she added, "I am in her hands, and
she may dispose of me as she will."

A few days later the French envoy sent from Charles IX

was shocked to find her gloomy apartment at Carlisle under strict surveillance by Elizabeth's soldiers. Even Mary Stuart was beginning to suspect she had merely fled from a Scottish captivity to an English one.

CHAPTER XX

AN INQUIRY — AND A PROPOSAL

ONE by one the friends who had accompanied Mary Stuart across the Border were sent upon their various ways, and by the middle of July she herself was transferred under strong guard to Bolton Castle in the Yorkshire moors. It is evident that even before her arrival there some sort of official trial had been decided upon. Elizabeth soon realized that an explanation must be offered to Europe for detaining a friendly Queen in custody — while Moray realized at long last that there must be serious extenuation for a Queen's dethronement. Melville, who by this time was evidently disgusted with Moray's manners — and morals too — declares that it was Cecil who chiefly influenced the Regent and "his least honest followers" to "accuse their native queen before the Queen and Council of England, to the great dishonor of their country and Prince."

The word *trial* was, of course, carefully avoided. For when the first suggestion of any official inquiry into her innocence reached Mary, she protested to Elizabeth: first that the latter had "admitted into her presence her bastard brother" while refusing that right to herself; next that she could and would cheerfully justify herself before her sister Queen, "but not in the form of a trial with my subjects, if they

149

bark at me with my hands tied. Madame, they and I are
not companions in anything!"

Mary had not only a picturesque and impassioned eloquence — she had also an excellent legal sense. Then and
throughout her entire imprisonment in England she insisted
that as an equal Queen who had come into the country of
her own free will she could not legally be detained, nor
could she be tried by English laws. So she begs Elizabeth
not to be her enemy if she will not be her friend; and to
suffer her to return to Scotland or to retire into France,
where she has a dowry for her maintainance. But her departure was the last thing either Elizabeth or Cecil wished.
So the Scottish Queen was assured that the ordeal would be
merely a series of friendly *conferences* or *inquiries,* with the
object of bringing out the truth and perhaps arbitrating the
difficulties between her and her subjects. As this sounded
reasonable, Mary consented to take part in them. That she
did not consider them of paramount importance seems
evident from the fact that at this time she was also praying
Elizabeth to use her influence in favor of the "poor prisoners" — Mary's loyal followers in Scotland — who were in
great danger from Moray's men. And she requested the
English Queen to take personal charge of her jewelry and
rings: accepting any she found to her own taste, but not permitting any more to be appropriated and sold by the Regent.
Naturally she could not know that the latter had already
sold to Elizabeth, at a suspiciously low price, one of her
most beautiful pearl necklaces.

In that same September Mary Stuart wrote to the Queen
of Spain — her childhood's devoted playmate, Madame Ysabel
— thanking her for the friendly and consoling letters which
seemed "as if sent from God to solace me amidst so many
troubles and adversities." She refers almost casually to
"losing the battle" of Langside after her eleven-month im-

prisonment at Lochleven, and to her present incarceration. But it is noticeable that neither here nor in any future communication, except under the gravest necessity, does she mention the name of Bothwell. Evidently she had determined to root him, and as far as possible his memory, from her life. However she does comment candidly upon Elizabeth's aiding "subjects against their princes," in spite of being herself "in some fear of insurrections." With her incorrigible optimism Mary adds: "God be praised, I believe I have gained the hearts of a great many good people in this country since my coming, so that they are ready to hazard all they possess for me and my cause." And her references to the religious situation are enlightening. "I must tell you that I am offered many fine things to change my religion, which I will never do," she protests to her old confidante: "but if I am compelled to yield in some points . . . it will be because I am a prisoner. Now I assure you, and beseech you to assure the king, that I shall die in the Roman Catholic religion, whatever they may say to the contrary." And wistfully, almost playfully, the outcast Queen of Scots refers to a matter Ysabel had evidently once mentioned — the possible future marriage of one of the latter's daughters to Mary's son James!

It is unlikely that this very significant letter was ever received by the Queen of Spain, as the latter died on October 3rd. When Mary Stuart heard the tragic news, along with other rumors in November, she wrote immediately to her "well beloved brother, cousin and ally," Philip II, telling him of her extreme grief on two counts. "One of these is that of the death of the Queen, your consort . . . the best sister and friend I had in the world . . . whose soul may God receive! And the other, that someone has represented to you that I am wavering in my religion, and that . . . you doubt, sometimes, whether I have any at all. . . . I know not which

of the two grieves me most." Once again the poor exile
pleads with the rigid Philip to remember her helplessness
as a prisoner among Protestants; once again she reiterates
her intention of "living and dying" in the Catholic Faith.

This correspondence reveals the inner struggle of Mary's
heart and soul at this time. But historically, of course, what
stands out during that autumn of 1568 was the opening at
York of the momentous "Inquiries." The English commissioners — to all intents the judges — included the Duke
of Norfolk, the Earl of Sussex, and that Sir Ralph Sadler
who had been ambassador to Scotland before and after
Mary's birth. With the Scottish Regent came a rare group
of the Queen's enemies and traducers: Morton, Maitland,
and Lindsay, that George Douglas who had been Darnley's
evil genius, the apostate Bishop of Orkney, who had married
her to Bothwell, and George Buchanan — the obscure Latin
scholar whom she had befriended and brought from France,
but who now found it more profitable to be on Moray's
side. Mary Stuart, not being permitted to appear in her own
defense, sent as her representatives the Lords Herries, Boyd,
Fleming, and Livingston, and John Leslie, the faithful if
not always prudent Bishop of Ross. These latter she had
already warned against spurious documents which might
be produced, demanding that she herself should have the
right to inspect and answer them. "For there are divers in
Scotland, both men and women, that can counterfeit my
handwriting," she declared, "and principally such as are in
company with themselves." This last phrase *gives furiously
to think,* as the French put it. For "in company with themselves" were not only the half brother with whom she had
been on such familiar terms, but her former secretary Maitland — husband of her cousin Mary Fleming — and the infamous Buchanan who had been her schoolmaster!

At the opening of the trial Mary Stuart's envoys rather

wisely took the offensive by putting in a detailed complaint against Moray's party. Morton and his companions they accused of deceiving Mary at Carberry Hill, imprisoning her at Lochleven, forcing her abdication, and usurping the Regency. Curiously enough, the Regent Moray, before putting up any defense or hinting at the contents of a certain precious casket in his possession, put several confidential questions to the English referees. He wanted to be assured what authority they would have to sentence the Scottish Queen if her guilt were proved — whether she might be delivered back into the hands of her own countrymen — and whether he and his followers could be certain of Elizabeth's support and protection. They were extraordinary questions to ask of supposedly neutral commissioners, and the latter seem at first to have resented them: probably they did not know the extent of the understanding between Moray and the English Queen, or that he was ready to hand over Dumbarton Castle in return for her help.

At any rate the Regent was evidently satisfied with his answers, for within a few days he came out with a public denial of all charges, attacking Bothwell and protesting that Mary Stuart had voluntarily abdicated her crown and appointed him Regent without his knowledge! Then, having a probable suspicion that these protestations would carry little weight, he committed an act of characteristic villainy. Without the knowledge of Mary's commissioners, he secretly had conveyed to the English judges a piece of evidence to be known as the "Casket Letters." For some months he, Morton, and Maitland had been planting rumors that such letters existed, although they seemingly found it difficult to agree just what story would best serve their purpose of blackening the Queen's reputation. To a modern, unprejudiced student the only unquestionably authentic thing in this whole dastardly business is the casket itself — a beautiful silver-gilt

box which had been presented to Mary by the loyal and
loving Dauphin François, and brought back by her to Scotland. According to one set of stories this little chest was
captured by some of the Scotch lords after her flight from
Holyrood or Lochleven. According to another it was taken
from Bothwell's servant Dalgleish, who was trying to convey
it to his master after Carberry Hill. As both Dalgleish, who
was supposed to have carried the letters, and Paris, the Bothwell page who was supposed to have seen them and testified
to their authenticity, had already been executed by the very
lords who now produced the casket, no contraditions need
be feared. But the accusers were a little long in deciding
upon its exact contents. At first they announced that it
contained letters from Queen Mary "written and subscrivit
[signed] by her own hand." By the time these were produced
at York there was no signature to any of them: probably
because, as Sir Edward Parry suggests,* to forge a letter
was a minor offense in Scottish law, while to forge a royal
signature might easily be construed as high treason. In any
case, the casket finally produced by Moray — admittedly it
had been in his possession over a year, during which time
there had been every opportunity for partial or complete
forgery — contained eight letters supposed to have been
written by Mary Stuart to Bothwell during the winter and
spring of 1567. Most of these were of a compromisingly
affectionate tone, while two paint the Queen as a confessed
accomplice in bringing Darnley to Edinburgh for his murder,
and others imply her knowledge of and collusion in the
abduction by Bothwell. For good measure there were also
two marriage contracts between Mary and Bothwell: one in
French and entirely undated; the other in Scotch, claimed to
be in Huntley's handwriting (which was, of course, never

————

* *The Persecution of Mary Stewart.*

corroborated), and dated April 5th — before the prospective groom's acquittal or the Ainsley Tavern bond. Added to all this was a series of "fond ballads" or so-called sonnets, of such banal sentimentality and in such wretched French that — it is consoling to know! — both Ronsard and Brantôme later declared Mary incapable of perpetrating them. It is more than significant that the odious Buchanan subsequently thought it worth while to transpose this drivel into Latin; for surely only their original author would have taken that trouble!

At first these letters must presumably have been presented in French: but Moray took care that the original drafts should disappear immediately after the trial; and the only surviving copies are either in Latin, English, or broad Scotch — the two latter languages in which the Queen was not yet able to write. In spite of this discrepancy, and the fact that the letters were not only *unsigned* but *undated* and *unaddressed,* they seem at first to have shocked the English commissioners, who reported upon them to Cecil: commenting particularly upon "a horrible long letter of her own hand, as they say, containing foul matter and abominable to be either thought of or to be written by a prince." (This was, of course, the 3000-word epistle Mary was supposed to have written the very night of her arrival in Glasgow to visit Darnley!) But their effect was not for long. During the week end, his Grace of Norfolk and Maitland had, Bishop Leslie tells us, "ridden and reasoned together" — with the result that the Duke became convinced Mary was being calumniated. As the greatest and richest peer in England, he did not hesitate to rebuke the Scotch lords for defaming their own Queen; even going so far as to declare that while he would "serve and honor" Elizabeth as long as she lived, he considered Mary Stuart next in order of succession to the English throne. And his companion Sussex wrote to Cecil on

October 22nd, advising against any public accusation of the Scottish Queen: "for that if her adverse party accuse her of the murder by producing of her letters, she will deny them, and accuse most of them of manifest consent to the murder, hardly to be denied; so as upon trial of both sides her proofs will judicially fall out best."

Realizing that the casket contents was not having the effect they had hoped, the Regent's men now produced not more proofs but more bitter and detailed accusations. Moray, Morton, Lindsay, the Bishop of Orkney, and the rest — without the cautious Maitland this time — came out with a written affidavit "boldly and constantly" affirming that Bothwell was "chief executor of the horrible and unworthy murder of King Henry of good memory," while the Queen was "of the foreknowledge, counsel, devise, persuader and commander thereto." In vain Mary Stuart issued from her prison impassioned denials, declaring the letters — which were their only proof and which she was not even allowed to see at first hand — to be forgeries; demanding the right to be heard in her own defense before Elizabeth and representatives of the neutral sovereigns of Europe.

Instead of answering, the English Queen — who may have been curious to read the Casket Letters herself or may have wished the whole proceedings to seem more important — ordered the "inquiry" transferred to London. Here, in the beautiful Camera Depicta of Westminster Hall, Cecil and the Earl of Leiscester were added to the commissioners and the tragic farce continued. Once again the casket contents was displayed, along with a new "eik," or accusation, of Mary's supposed crimes said to have been drawn up — with eloquence but without any objective proof — by Buchanan, who later embalmed his own infamy and incidentally perpetuated all the calumnies against Mary Stuart in the Latin of his *Detectio*.

One of the few decent moments of this mock trial was when Lord Herries rose to deliver the famous "harangue" in which he berated his countrymen for trying to color falsely their own "most unjust, ingrate and shameful doings." He was himself a soldier rather than a lawyer, but his arraignment of these nobles whom the Queen had raised to their present eminence was masterful. He explained scornfully and in detail how, early in her reign, Mary, "being of herself, as is well known, a liberal princess, gave them in her youth for their unshamefaced begging . . . two parts of the patrimony pertaining to the crown of Scotland." This unwise prodigality was only possible because Mary Stuart had her own French dowry to draw on for her personal support. But coming into "further years and greater understanding," she realized that her heir and his royal successors would not be able to "maintain their estate" upon this third part of their patrimony; so she determined to take advantage of an old law by which rulers could undo official acts before their twenty-fifth year. It was, Herries continued, in fear of this withdrawal of their estates that the jealous lords conspired first against her adviser, Rizzio. Next, "seeing her son an infant not a year old, they could find no better way than to cut off their sovereign liege lady" — hoping, of course, for a long regency and continuation of their booty.

Being unable to answer these charges, Moray's lords rose in a clamor, declaring that Herries had "lied in his throat" — an Elizabethan challenge he promptly returned. Only the efforts of the English Queen and Mary's representative, the Bishop of Ross, prevented a duel. Once more the Scottish Queen's commissioners put in a plea to produce their own chief witness: when this was again refused, they withdrew upon her orders from the whole futile "Inquiry." By this time Elizabeth and Cecil seem to have decided the trial had gone far enough, and it was ended upon a note of typically English compromise. Moray and his men might retain the government of Scotland, since nothing had been demonstrated "that might impair their honor or allegiance." On the other hand, nothing had been "sufficiently proven or shown by them against the Queen their sovereign, whereby the Queen of England should conceive or take any evil opinion of her good sister for anything yet seen." Both sides had brought charges of murder and treachery, yet both sides were equally acquitted!

So everybody went home except the star-crossed Queen of Scots. For her own "safety," and awaiting some not-impossible future evidence — which, of course, never arrived until Cecil and Walsingham created it eighteen years later — she was to remain in the custody of her good sister Elizabeth. Meanwhile the seeds of calumny had been sown: they could be left to bear their sinister fruit down the byways and down the centuries. "I am in your power," wrote Mary to her cousin: but she trusted in "God, and time, the father of truth," for vindication.*

The inquiry had seemed to end on a note of complete anticlimax. But its real climax came as a by-product. Early in the year 1569 the Duke of Norfolk, Earl Marshall of England and chief of her former judges, loomed up as suitor for the hand of Mary Stuart.

---

* NOTE: To the present author, and to most other people familiar with modern judicial methods, it seems unnecessary to delve deeply into the old and futile controversy of the Casket Letters. For written evidence which is never shown to the defendant, and the original of which conveniently disappears immediately after a trial, automatically rules itself out from respect or credence. Any reader who is further interested in the subject of the forgeries will find them exhaustively discussed in *An Examination of the Letters Said to be Written by Mary Queen of Scots to James Earl of Bothwell*, by Walter Goodall. Copies of the letters are also published — and dismissed — in Herbert Gorman's *The Scottish Queen*.

CHAPTER XXI

BRIEF CANDLE . . .

Never was a man more the confused child of his confused age than this Thomas Howard, Fourth Duke of Norfolk. His grandfather, the Third Duke, left an unforgettable comment on what Reformation and Renaissance had already begun to mean in his classic remark: "It was merry in England before the New Learning." This man's son — the father of Mary's Duke — was that Henry Howard, Earl of Surrey, who will always have a place in the hearts of poetry lovers because, along with his friend Sir Thomas Wyatt, he brought the Italian love sonnet to England. When he quite rightly urged the claims of his father, Norfolk, instead of the brutal Somerset as Regent to young Edward VI, he was promptly beheaded — leaving the eleven-year-old son Thomas. This boy, having been brought up in the Old Faith, was now placed under the tutorship of that Foxe who later produced his very Protestant *Book of Martyrs*. In spite of this, the youth seems to have been popular at the court of Mary Tudor. Having succeeded to the Dukedom of Norfolk upon his grandfather's death in 1554, he was later courted by Elizabeth, who conferred on him the Knighthood of the Garter. And although he was then only twenty-three years old, that Queen put him in charge of the army she sent to Scotland to assist the Lords of the Congregation against the dying Marie de Guise and her French troops. By this time Norfolk, like many another Englishman of his time, can scarcely have known what his own religion was. But apparently he did not relish the Scottish mission, and after signing a pact with Châtelheraut he was glad to return to England. That he loved beauty is evident from the fact that he built the Charterhouse as his home and helped in the completion of Magdalen College at Oxford. It is also evident that he had particularly sad luck in his marriages; for when the Queen of Scots fled to England in 1568 he was a widower for the third time.

He was then in his thirty-third year, and just when he first met Mary Stuart is uncertain. In fact, there is no documentary proof of their meeting at all. But all the northern nobility — particularly those of Catholic leanings — seem to have flocked to her at Carlisle; where she remained about two months under the guardianship of Norfolk's sister, Lady Scrope. However he gave no special evidence of any predilection for the Scottish Queen until the iniquitous Inquiries of York and Westminister, where she was never allowed to appear in her own defense.

During the year 1569 Elizabeth was becoming more and more involved in the foolish and futile negotiations for her own marriage with the young Duke of Anjou — later Henri III of France — and for awhile she either did not know or did not care much about Norfolk's proposal to the Queen of Scots. If one forgets that the Duke had obtained an English grant of £500 for Moray, and also headed off an attack upon him by the Scottish lords when he returned after the trial, it may seem strange that the Regent pretended for awhile to favor his suit. Maitland, who now repented the betrayal of his Queen, was probably sincere in his own approval of the match. But why Elizabeth's favorite, Leicester, should also encourage the project is less easily understood — unless he cleverly foresaw that it might cause the downfall of Norfolk, who had evidently snubbed him. Apparently the Duke's idea was to achieve Mary Stuart's liberation and return to her Scottish throne; and after Elizabeth's death to unite the two kingdoms under the rule of Mary or her son. He was a visionary politician, changeable, and not too efficient at best. But after all, he was the son of a poet and a political martyr. And he was merely anticipating what history brought to pass after he and Mary had both lost their lives.

Her own attitude toward the proposed marriage seems to have been a pathetic and somewhat desperate clutching at a straw. "I look for good will and constancy again!" she exclaimed in the first letter to Norfolk which has survived; but also she warned him against Moray's enmity. And she evidently stipulated that the nullity of the Bothwell union — which everybody, including Bothwell himself, who was being sued by his first wife in Denmark, now conceded — should be established; and that Norfolk should return to his ancestral Faith. This he seemed quite ready to do, and for awhile the whole vertiginous vision appeared capable of becoming reality.

It may have been because of Elizabeth's growing suspicions that the Queen of Scots was suddenly — and cruelly, for she was ill and it was in the heart of February — removed from Bolton Castle to Tutbury in Staffordshire, under the care of the Earl of Shrewsbury and his wife, Bess of Hardwick. The place was abominably cold and unsanitary and became the most hated of all her prisons. But that Mary's vital charm was not yet impaired by hardship is evident from the report of a young Irishman, Nocholas White, sent to visit her there at Cecil's request. After the usual polite assurance that the royal prisoner was "not comparable" to Elizabeth, he describes the former as having "an alluring grace, a pretty Scottish accent and a searching wit, crowned with mildness.

Fame might move some to relieve her, and glory joined to gain might stir others to venture much for her sake. . . . Mine own affection, by seeing the Queen's Majesty is doubled, and thereby I guess what she might work on others." Reading between the lines of this somewhat ingenuous report it is impossible not to suspect that "the old fox" Cecil was already on the trail of Norfolk. But White's final lines are a contribution to one of the many mysteries of Mary Stuart's life — the device or motto she kept for so many years and even in prison upon her royal canopy. "In looking upon her cloth of estate," he reports, "I noticed this sentence embroidered, *En ma fin est mon commencement,* which is a riddle I understand not."

In April, probably because her royal cousins in France had been protesting her imprisonment, Queen Mary was transferred to another home of the Shrewsburys, Wingfield Manor. Here she was more comfortable, and could return to her reading and embroidery; while Lady Shrewsbury, always a reckless talker, seems to have regaled the hours with many a scandalous tale of Elizabeth's doings.

The English Queen was even more than usually tempestuous that spring and summer. Either hysterically or for political effect she injected a new note into the Anjou affair by charging she had heard rumors that Mary Stuart had previously, with the consent of the Pope, ceded to Henri her rights to the English throne, which he might claim at any time. Young Anjou — who was eighteen years Elizabeth's junior and secretly detested her — wrote that such a cession "had never been made . . . nor thought of; nor has it been approved by Our Holy Father the Pope; neither have we ever had any will nor intention of any war or invasion of the said Queen of England." What Elizabeth probably had in mind — if she was not just trying to stir up dust against other activities — was the fact that before

Mary's marriage to François, back in 1558, she had ceded
her rights to the *Scottish* throne to her father-in-law, Henri
II, in case she should die childless: all of which was, of
course, nullified by the subsequent birth of her son James.

But in a few months the Tudor Queen had a chance for
one of her characteristic rages when Norfolk appeared at
court and admitted that he had dared, without her consent,
to dream of marrying Mary Stuart. She had him promptly
imprisoned in the Tower to think matters over — and had
poor Mary returned to Tutbury.

Presently the Scottish Queen sent Elizabeth a letter, in
strictest harmony with the international law of the time,
again asking permission that she might retire to France
among her friends and allies; or else that she might redeem
herself "by ransom, as is the custom of all prisoners, even
those who are enemies." But the plea went unanswered. For
in that very month of November, the Earls of Northumberland and Westmoreland — knowing Tutbury to be ill de-
fended — led an abortive uprising to rescue Mary. Unfortunately Cecil had news of the movement, and Mary was
temporarily removed to the Bull Inn at Coventry. The whole
enterprise was avenged with great brutality upon the rank
and file; and while its leaders escaped across the Border,
Northumberland eventually paid the price with his head.
Like all unsuccessful uprisings it led to extra harshness
against its object; for Elizabeth realized increasingly that
the older nobility of England resented Mary Stuart's confinement and favored her as next in line of succession.

Back at Tutbury, Mary seems to have suffered in both
spirit and body. In fact, from now on she refers often to her
illnesses — to a dry cough, a cold in the eye, and that persistent pain in the side: "for my imprisonment makes me
unwell." But the young year 1570 brought some hope along
with it. Several times since her arrival in England the Queen

of Scots had written to the Holy Father, Pius V, declaring her devotion to the Catholic Church and imploring full reconciliation with the Papacy. On January 9th he issued a brief restoring her to favor, sympathizing with her misfortunes and holding out hopes of aid through France and Spain. For her comfort he even quoted Christ's beatitude *for those who suffer persecution for justice's sake.* After all, no one understands human frailty like the saints, and Pius was to be numbered among them.

The consolation of this papal message must have been full of healing to Mary, bruised by the knowledge that since her banishment the beautiful chapel of Holyrood House had been sacked and all public offices of the Church suspended throughout her kingdom. It meant, too, that from time to time she might now expect the ministrations of a chaplain, even if the priest had to come in disguise.

On a lower level but inevitably cheering was another piece of news arriving about this time. This was the shooting of her most inveterate enemy, Moray, by one of the Hamilton clan, at Linlithgow. To Bishop Leslie she wrote that while she had had no knowledge of the plot she could not help rejoicing in its success. A few days later, her ever tender heart persuaded her to send another letter to Moray's widow, declaring: "Albeit your late husband had so unnaturally and unthankfully offended us . . . we desired not his bloodshed . . . but maun be sorry for his death." In point of fact her bastard brother's passing did not greatly help Mary, since he was succeeded as Regent by Darnley's father, Lennox — until, two years later, Lennox too was assassinated by the Scottish lords.

With the coming of spring the Queen was moved from her hated Tutbury to a new prison at Chatsworth — and the Duke of Norfolk was liberated from the Tower. A few months before Mary had written to him: "If you and I could escape both, we should find friends enough. . . . You have promised to be mine and I yours; I believe the Queen of England and country should like of it. . . ." adding her intention to do nothing that would endanger him or without his advice, and signing herself delightfully:

"Your own, faithful to death, Queen of Scots, my Norfolk."

Before long her optimistic belief that Elizabeth would approve her union with Norfolk was shattered, so both he and she began to concentrate upon plans for her own escape. England, like all countries where a vital minority is held in political subjection, bristled with plots and counterplots — most of them quite impossible of fulfillment. One of the most grandiose was launched during 1570 by one Rudolphi or Ridolfi, an Italian long resident in London, who — no doubt encouraged by the English Catholic nobility — went so far as to visit the Pope and Philip II seeking a naval expedition to rescue the Queen of Scots and place her on the throne. Naturally the Holy Father neither could nor would do anything about such an enterprise. And Philip, as usual, temporized and procrastinated. He wanted to help the royal Catholic prisoner and at the same time to avenge English attacks upon his shipping, but even more he dreaded to throw Elizabeth any further into the arms of Anjou and France.

Meanwhile Mary was far from thinking only of herself: in fact her letters are eloquent proof of how much she thought about other people. She worried keenly because her son was being brought up in "impiety" and taught slanderous lies about her by his grandfather, Lennox. To her ambassador in France, the Bishop of Glasgow, she writes feelingly upon the death of his brother, her faithful servitor John Beaton; and more than once she urges him — even at the sacrifice of some of her French property — to see that funds are given to young George Douglas, who had aided her flight from Lochleven and was then in France. "I would not for the world neglect things which concern . . . my duty to God and my honour," she protests. And although the plea to *make one last effort for your Queen* runs like an aching undertone through all this correspondence, she does not forget to suggest that if a certain young Protestant Gordon who carried one of her letters could have a Jesuit instructor, he might easily be converted. In this same missive she begs that King Charles IX will obtain a confessor for herself — "to administer the sacraments in case God should call me by one way or another."

Like most people who write well and enjoy writing, Mary Stuart wrote far too much. As she had both the gift of words and a definitely legal turn of mind, it was quite natural that she should have drawn up and conveyed to Norfolk a carefully detailed "memorandum" of Rudolphi's fantastic plans for an invasion of England. It was all natural enough: but Norfolk was never a prudent person, and the papers he did not destroy fell eventually into Cecil's hands. So in the September of 1571 Elizabeth stopped long enough in her toying with Anjou to send the Duke back again to the Tower — this time under a charge of treason.

The brief candle of Mary's last romance was flickering to its death.

CHAPTER   XXII

THE IRON CURTAIN

FROM this time on Mary Stuart's drama was played out behind a more and more tightly clamped iron curtain. It was a long Way of the Cross with many separate Stations, for she was moved from prison to prison — Tutbury, Chatsworth, Sheffield, Chartley — for no very intelligible reason, before the final Calvary of Fotheringay was reached. More than once the body broke under the strain and her life was despaired of: more than once it found temporary relief in some new interest or in the healing baths at Buxton. But it is impossible not to conclude that she was being reserved for martyrdom.

As few visitors were permitted to see the Queen of Scots during these fifteen years, the progress of her misery must be gauged chiefly by what happened in the stormy world outside or by the flash of some personal reaction lighting the pages of letters which have managed to survive. 1572 was a year heavy with tragedy. In June both Norfolk and the Earl of Northumberland were beheaded by Elizabeth's orders. In August, Catherine de Medici, having encouraged the Huguenots so long that she was known as "the Protestant Queen," found that they were becoming too powerful politically. So the horror of the St. Bartholomew's Day Massacre took the life of Coligny and bathed Paris in blood

— bringing its inevitably bitter reaction against the Catholic
Counter-Reformation which was beginning to bear fruit
all over Europe. Up in Scotland the Civil War stormed on,
with King's Lords, Queen's Lords, and Lords on their own
fighting one another. The Earl of Mar, who had succeeded
to the Regency after Lennox's assassination, proved the exception by dying of natural causes. But when his post was
taken over by the brutal and unscrupulous Morton, it was
not long before Kirkaldy of Grange was murdered and Maitland of Lethington — both of whom had returned to Mary
Stuart's allegiance and attempted to hold Edinburgh Castle
for her — died under suspicion of poisoning. Ironically
enough it was at this very moment, with his friend and
champion Morton in command of Scotland, that John Knox
was called to give his final crooked reckoning. Under date
of November 24, 1572, the curious and usually laconic
Scottish register, the *Diurnal of Remarkable Occurrents,*
carried a new entry: "John Knox, minister, deceased, who
had, as was alleged, the most part of the blame of all the sor-
rows of Scotland since the slaughter of the late Cardinal."
It was a rather overpowering arraignment.

Glimpses which filter through the captive Queen's letters
and other reports during the early part of 1574 are a little
more comforting and show how indomitably Mary was
seeking some adjustment to her death-in-life. Her jailors,
Lord and Lady Shrewsbury, had almost, if temporarily, become her friends. A visiting chaplain was occasionally
smuggled in; and Bess of Hardwick's granddaughter brought
a breath of youth into her devotion to Mary and her sharing
of the royal bedchamber. In spite of a chronic rheumatism
and other symptoms growing out of "cold and lack of
exercise," the Scottish Queen kept busy with her needle as
well as her pen. She began a friendly correspondence with
Darnley's mother, Lady Lennox, and wrote in detail to

Archbishop Beaton and Thomas Morgan (formerly a secretary of Shrewsbury's) about the management of her dwindling and evidently neglected French dowry. And probably in a final hope of placating Elizabeth — with whom she was still seeking that interview which would clear away all misunderstandings! — she sent the latter embroidered headdresses and other pieces of her beautiful handiwork, which may well have seemed coals of fire to the guilty recipient.

In May of that year young Charles IX died, miserably and fearfully as he had lived, and the Duke of Anjou came to the French throne as Henri III. This, of course, brought to a close the long talks of his marriage with Queen Elizabeth — who, a few years later, was to begin far more passionate overtures to his still younger brother Hercule. And as Henri was, with all his perversities, a more dynamic person than Charles had ever been, his advent inspired Mary Stuart with fresh hopes of freedom. There is something of the old coquetry in her request to her patient French ambassador to send to Sheffield dress patterns of silk and cloth of silver, crown headdresses "such as were formerly made for me"; also some new-fashioned veils and ribbons from Italy — "for though I do not wear such myself, they will be put to a better purpose." And it was very much part of Mary Stuart's nature to beg for some turtledoves and Barbary fowls, which would be "amusement for a prisoner"; and for several "pretty little dogs," which must be sent very warmly wrapped in baskets. "For beside writing and work," she adds in lines that shake the heart, "I take pleasure only in all the little animals that I can get."

Two more deaths were bound to strike Mary close. At the end of 1574 came that of her girlhood's mentor, the Cardinal of Lorraine. "Alas, I am a prisoner, and God has bereft me of one of those I most loved: what shall I say more?" she wrote when the news came — and the blot of her tears stains the letter to this day. Of the death of Bothwell in Denmark in 1576 Mary had only indirect word; for Elizabeth hid from her the fact that he had left a long Declaration and a short Second Statement, both citing the many treacheries of the Scottish lords in their conspiracies against Rizzio and Darnley, and declaring her own total innocence and ignorance of the latter's death. It is important to remember that this "deathbed confession" of Bothwell — which has raised controversy, although it was endorsed by the Protestant lords and a Lutheran bishop in Denmark — finally admitted his own share in the Darnley murder, along with Morton, Moray, *et al.*, and was part of the evidence at the trial which later condemned Morton to death. And it is intriguing to note that in this same strange paper the Earl confessed that he had used "witchcraft and the inventions belonging thereunto" in winning the Queen's consent to marry him. Perhaps he believed he had, since the times were full of such superstition. But Mary never thought it necessary to look for magic in the tragic story of that seduction, nor need her defenders.

History records no comment of the unhappy Queen when the news of James Hepburn's death finally reached her. But Shrewsbury, her sympathetic jailor, reports after another shock that "She makes little show of grief, and yet it nips her very near." Evidently the former quick tears and the tendency to tense hysteria were yielding to the control of a will being steeled by frustration and mortal danger. About this same time there was secret agitation for her marriage with Don John of Austria — the heroic Spanish bastard whom Chesterton saluted as "the last knight of Europe": a union that from romantic and even apostolic angles might have been the fulfillment of her destiny and the revolutionizing of Europe's. When news of his death came in 1578, we know only that Mary slipped into silence and touched no food for two days. But from her letters we know a good deal about her urging the faithful Mary Seaton, who had been allowed to join her at Sheffield, to wed the equally loyal young Andrew Beaton; until he, too, met a sudden death in France.

Death was, indeed, a close neighbor to everyone in the sixteenth century. But to Mary Stuart treason and an often futile cruelty were even closer. One instance of the latter was the fact that during her long imprisonment she had to be constantly appealing for a chaplain — although even the diplomatic representatives of Catholic countries were allowed that courtesy in London. Another is the petty and ignoble way in which all intercourse between the Queen and her young son was surreptitiously held up. In 1579 Mary sent her new secretary Claude Nau — a Frenchman later proved to be also in the pay of Elizabeth — all the way to Scotland with a letter, some jewels, and a little vest she had personally embroidered for the boy. But since she addressed him as Prince rather than King of Scotland, her messenger was sent away without being allowed to enter his presence. For this Morton must probably shoulder the blame: but either Cecil or the English Queen herself must answer for the fact that the youth's reply was never permitted to reach his mother. This somewhat naïve epistle, "To the Queen of Scotland, my very honoured dame," assures her that it was not according to his good will that her secretary was dismissed, and that he received the ring she had sent and would take great care of it in her honor. He sends her one of his own in return, protesting his love and obedience and even craving her advice. A postscript in the boy's own hand shows how much of a child James was in spite of his thirteen years: "Madame," he writes, "I commend to you the fidelity of my little ape, who never stirs from me. I will often send you news of us."

One can imagine what comfort and what a smile this letter would have brought to the lonely heart of Mary Stuart — if it had been allowed to reach Sheffield instead of being locked away in Elizabeth's State Paper Office.

CHAPTER   XXIII

PLOTS – AND COUNTERPLOTS

IN JUNE, 1581, the Regent Morton was, after many accusations and a brief trial, decapitated in Edinburgh for the murder of King Henry Darnley. So ended the last of the Scottish triumvirate who had planned Mary's downfall; and so, as it seemed, must end the calumnies which had persistently linked her name with their own crimes. The Queen herself believed Morton at this time her "greatest enemy" and rejoiced in the brighter prospects she dreamed ahead. There was, indeed, some plausible fact beneath the dream. Young Esmé Stuart, a first cousin of Darnley and friend of the Duc de Guise, was now the strongest influence on the fifteen-year-old King James. And while as unreliable as he was attractive, and never quite certain whether to declare himself Catholic or Protestant, he seemed at first to favor the union of mother and son in Scotland, with French help if needed. The Jesuits, Father Parsons and Father Creighton, arrived in Paris with detailed plans for a joint reign of Mary and James – which might have been an excellent and workable idea. It met with the approval of Mary herself, of Pope Gregory, and of Spanish Philip. And the Duc de Guise could probably have added the approval of France: although this was temporarily delayed because Elizabeth was at the height of her fatuous and

pathetic courtship by — or rather of — the boyish Duke
d'Alençon, who had succeeded his brother Henri as Duke
of Anjou. Hercule was believed to be Protestant at heart:
he and the English Queen had kissed in public and some
sort of marriage contract seems actually to have been drawn
up. And poor Elizabeth was so foolishly enamored that she
apparently extended her infatuation and her favors to the
Duke's emissary, Monsieur de Semier — somewhat to the
scandal of her not easily scandalized court.

By all counts Mary Stuart should have been in better favor
in England at this time, as she had finally consented to sign
the long-disputed Treaty of Edinburgh: with the single but
important reservation that she should never relinquish her
rights as heir apparent to the English throne if Elizabeth
died childless. But those who planned for a peaceful solution of the long impasse between the two countries were
counting without the persistent jealousy of the Scottish lords
and its equally persistent encouragement by Cecil. Just as
a solution seemed in sight, the boy King was kidnaped by
that implacable Earl of Ruthven who had persecuted his
Queen at Lochleven and whose sardonic father had led the
murderers of Rizzio. To Mary this blow was of the cruelest,
and it induced one of the most critical illnesses of her final
years. At Sheffield she and those about her believed she
could not recover — a catastrophe which contemporary comments indicate would have been highly welcome to the
English court.

But recover she did. And by November, 1582, she was
able to write Elizabeth one of the most eloquent and deeply
moving letters of her career. "Madame," it begins, "upon
that which has come to my knowledge of the last conspiracies executed in Scotland against my poor child, having
reason to fear the consequence of it from the example of
myself, I must employ the very small remainder of my life

and strength before my death to discharge my heart to you fully. . . ." There is a note not less then awesome in the simplicity with which Mary, in the name of the living God and "before Him sitting between you and me," reminds Elizabeth of the endless line of "spies and secret messengers" sent to corrupt her Scotch subjects while she was still on the throne — of Throckmorton's assurance at Lochleven that her abdication would be invalid because forced — of her arrest in England and the unjust captivity through which she has already suffered "a thousand deaths." She recalls that the Norfolk episode was "sanctioned with the advice and signatures" of the highest members of Elizabeth's council and of her own, including Leicester, Moray, and Maitland. But it is the fact that she has been cut off from all communication with her son, who hears no word of her except evil from those whose advantage it is to separate them, which draws Mary Stuart's most burning words. "By what right," she demands, "can it be maintained that I, the mother of my child, am totally prohibited not only from assisting him in his urgent necessity, but also from having any intelligence of his state? . . . I cannot, Madame, endure it any longer. . . . The vilest criminals that are in your prisons, born under your obedience, are admitted to their justification, and their accusers and their accusations are always declared to them. Why, then, shall not the same order have place toward me, a sovereign queen, your nearest relative and lawful heir?" Mary's pen paused a moment as she remembered that it was this very affinity of blood and royalty which had caused the enmity between her and Elizabeth, and she protested that she looked no longer for any kingdom but that of God, who seemed to be preparing the end of her adversities. Then she broke into the last heartbreaking plea: "For the sake of the painful passion of our Saviour and Redeemer, Jesus Christ, again I supplicate you to permit

me to withdraw myself out of your realm into some place
of repose, to seek comfort for my poor body . . . that with
liberty of conscience I may prepare my soul for God, who
is daily calling for it." Once again the prisoner begs that
"I may have with me for my consolation some honest
Churchman, to remind me daily of the course which I have
to finish and to teach me how to complete it conformably
with my religion, in which I am firmly resolved to live and
die. . . . Redeem the old pledges of your good nature. . . .
Let me have the satisfaction before I die of seeing all matters
happily settled between us. . . .

> Your very disconsolate nearest kinswoman and
> affectionate cousin, Mary, R."

The French original of this letter remains in the British
Museum, still bearing that "perpetual testimony" which
Mary Stuart prayed it might, of her case before Elizabeth
and before posterity. If the English Queen had given it the
answer it deserved, the record of history might well have
been changed for her as for her victim. For what Mary
Stuart asked was not mercy but simple justice. As Queen
Mother in Scotland, surrounded by envious lords, or as
Dowager in France under the surveillance of a none-too-
friendly court, she could scarcely be conceived as a menace
to anybody. And the matter of the English succession would
have passed on peacefully to her son James — as she had
predicted at his birth and as eventually happened. It was
Elizabeth's unjust and criminal insistence upon keeping
Mary a prisoner that focused attention upon her not as
deposed Queen of Scots but as potential Queen of England,
and consequently a rallying point for the frustrated Catholics
of the realm. And Mary herself, denied now all hope of
liberation by her sister Queen, felt and indeed was justified
both legally and ethically in seeking freedom by any means
offered. To be sure, these means were not very wise ones:

she had never been very wise in choosing methods or men. And she was pushed to desperation — an ill and aging woman, who saw liberty and the crown she still believed a divine gift being stolen from her son as they had been from herself.

Elizabeth, too, was becoming more and more desperate and disenchanted. In 1584 that which might well have been considered her final fling at romance — for who could have anticipated the late and tragic adventure with Essex? — was ended by the death of the young Duke of Anjou. She was past fifty, still inordinately vain and passionate, with what looks she once had hopelessly gone and what health she once had hopelessly weakened. Her reign was to be written down as one of the greatest in English history: yet she herself never felt secure upon her throne until she was within sight of losing it by death. She knew that in the Catholic judgment — that is to say, the traditional judgment of Christendom — she was illegitimate and excommunicate and a usurper. Therefore it was necessary to weaken this Catholic verdict by every means possible. Families of the Old Religion had already been robbed of lands and fortune, they were ineligible to enter the universities they had built or to hold any public office in the kingdom. The laity were subject to constant fines for recusancy (nonattendance at Protestant worship), the Mass was outlawed, and any Englishman who was ordained priest and returned to his country for more than forty days was subject to death for treason. Yet she and Cecil and Walsingham were haunted increasingly by the phoenix-resurgence of the Faith they had believed stamped out. They knew that the young apostles trained at Douai kept coming back, with shining faces set for martyrdom: that the sons of Ignatius, under myriad disguises, were dispensing secret sacraments in dark upper rooms of London and the English countryside. They knew, too, that Philip would not forever suffer the pillage of his ships and his colonies — that France and Scotland, weary of civil war, were not ignorant of the English money which persistently supported it. And they knew that to all these disaffected ones, at home and abroad, the symbol of a possible new hope — of what today might be called a *new deal* — was the imprisoned Queen of Scots. Knowing, they feared and hated all the more intensely.

There is no doubt that five years before her execution, the English Government had decided that Mary must die and that her death must be made to seem not martyrdom but just retribution. Regicide was, of course, in the air: William of Orange was its victim in 1584 and Henri III of France followed in 1589; and Elizabeth so feared the theme of Shakespeare's *Richard II* — showing the dethronement and execution of one of her own predecessors — that she would never permit its full performance while she lived. And this hysteria found expression in one law after another. The Statute of Silence made it a criminal offense in England even to discuss the next heir to the throne. And the notorious Bond of Association for the Safety of the Queen's Royal Person was a two-edged sword aimed directly at the throat of Mary Stuart. For beneath a thick wrapping of ambiguous and pious words it not only extended permission to "persecute to the death" anyone who had contrived a plot against Elizabeth including "anything compassed or imagined to this end." It also declared the person *in whose favor* such a conspiracy should be "imagined" equally guilty, with his or her heirs "excluded and disabled forever" from claiming the English crown. This meant, of course, a potential death sentence against Mary and exclusion of her son from the succession if somebody, even without her consent or knowledge, should contrive a plan to make her Queen of England!

But neither this witch-hunt at home nor the fact that Walsingham's *gestapo* was known to have half a hundred spies on the Continent served to discourage the epidemic of generally quite impotent plots and counterplots. By making English life unbearable to a large and impassioned minority, it rather encouraged them. Indeed — although there were plenty of real conspiracies, some urged by conscience and some by ambition — it was part of Cecil's policy to foment these intrigues for the sake of publicizing and then punishing them. For instance, that Dr. Parry, described as a "ruined" English courtier, who in 1584 sued Pope Gregory for an indulgence or blessing upon his hazy enterprise for the "liberation of the Queen of Scotland" and other unspecified Catholic benefits, was simply a Protestant agent of Cecil and Elizabeth. Most unwisely, and in spite of his own nuncio's warning that the man was probably a spy, the Pope granted this favor. So Parry returned to England to report the whole proceedings and be generously rewarded.

Such was the general situation when Mary found herself moved back to Tutbury, to enter perhaps the most tangled and tortured period of her career. There seems to have been almost nothing she was spared, in public or private grief, during the few remaining years. Her son James had escaped from the custody of Ruthven and sent the latter to the block. Then, with a duplicity reminiscent of his father, Darnley, he proceeded to hold out his left hand to Mendoza, the capable Spanish ambassador, and to his Guise cousins, with their promise of possible rescue for his mother — but his right hand to Elizabeth, with her prospect of the English succession and a present pension which he badly needed. Mary tried by every means to enter into a bond by which he should legally recognize her queenhood, and she should then transfer the kingdom of Scotland to him. Hearing rumors of his secret emissaries to Elizabeth, she protested: "I know the child doth love me and will not deal with the Queen without my advice."

Even after learning that two of his envoys had arrived in London, she remained hopeful. But before long her secretary Nau brought information that the time-serving young King was not merely treating independently with Elizabeth and accepting her pension of £5000: he had also turned informer against those loyal Scots who still conspired to free his mother, and he had omitted her name entirely when signing a treaty between England, France, and Scotland. In a frenzy of disappointed love and pride Mary wrote to the French ambassador, Mauvissière, that she was "wounded and cut to the heart" by the impiety and ingratitude her son had been "constrained" to commit against her. She threatened to invoke the malediction of God upon him; and pathetically enough, since she confessed herself "held captive in a desert," she threatened to disinherit James — who had already disinherited her! What she could not realize was that he was no longer a child, that he was his father's son, and that nothing in his training had encouraged love or loyalty to her. In March Mary Stuart sent to Elizabeth a letter which seems not to have received its full weight of importance from most historians. In it she declared that, as her insistence upon protecting her rights to the English succession had been for James rather than herself, she was now willing to "quit forever" those claims if the Queen would arrange a treaty permitting her to retire out of England into "some solitary place, as much for the repose of my soul as my body." But Elizabeth had, of course, far more final and far-reaching plans for disposing of her rival, and they were fast mounting to their climax.

As so often happens in the human story, the pinprick was persistently added to Mary's martyrdom. One of these superfluous blows came during that same 1584, when Bess of Hardwick, the Earl of Shrewsbury's wife, turned unpredictably from friend to enemy: and, as usual, political ambition and personal jealousy contributed to the change. For by her first marriage to Lord Cavendish, Bess had borne a daughter who in turn married Darnley's brother, Lennox; and these two, dying early, left a young child named Arabella Stuart. It seems suddenly to have occurred to Lady Shrewsbury that this granddaughter had a possible claim to the English throne — a claim naturally superseded by that of Queen Mary and her son. So, having for a long time been on stormy terms with her husband, the flighty woman determined to attack him and Mary Stuart together with accusations of undue intimacy. These were patently absurd, of course; and when the much-suffering Queen of Scots heard this new calumny she rose in magnificent wrath, faced Bess of Hardwick, threatened to reveal her scurrilous gossip about the English Queen, and forced a complete retraction. But the harm had been done, and never again could she and the reluctant Shrewsbury live peacefully as prisoner and jailor. He was evidently weary of the whole situation, and begged Elizabeth to be relieved of it — complaining incidentally of his "wicked and malicious wife." He was replaced by Sir Ralph Sadler, who was not unkindly disposed toward Mary: and after the French ambassador had again protested against Tutbury, the Queen of Scots and her pitiful following — the maids, the secretaries, the faithful physician, and the devoted little dogs — were removed before winter to Chartley, a property of the Earl of Essex. But soon, for a new penance, she saw Sadler succeeded as jailor by Sir Amias Poulet, a parsimonious Puritan and intimate of the crafty Walsingham. "The indisposition of this Queen's body, and the great infirmity of her legs, is no small advantage to her keeper," he wrote frigidly to London; adding that he need not have much fear of her running away if he could foresee that she should not be taken by force! He might have added, although the official wigs of the day probably hid the fact from his knowledge, that the red-brown Stuart hair was already white as wool.

CHAPTER XXIV

BABINGTON—AND WALSINGHAM

L ATER events proved that Sir Amias' conscience balked at the personal, private murder of his prisoner. But he evidently took a certain sadistic pleasure in heaping small humiliations upon her, and had no scruple in forwarding the cleverly contrived plot by which she was soon to be lured into self-betrayal and the official death sentence. For at Chartley a new Judas came into Mary's life. This was Gilbert Gifford, quondam seminarian of his brother's college at Rheims — a personable and guileless-faced young Englishman, who seems to have lost simultaneously both faith and honor. Just when or why he conceived the design of selling the Queen of Scots is one of the more sinister mysteries of history. But in France he had insinuated himself into the confidence of her agent Thomas Morgan and her ambassador Archbishop Beaton: and when he presented himself to Walsingham with a diabolically clever scheme for betraying Mary Stuart into his hands, he was naturally welcomed with vigorous if veiled cordiality. As a result of this interview, Gifford was soon installed in London lodgings with a hench-man of Walsingham's — one Thomas Phelippes, a counter-feiter of handwriting and expert at cipher-reading. This creature evidently saw to it that nobody should know much about him; but the description that comes down of the low-

statured, skulking man, "slender every way," pock-marked
and short-sighted, suggests Romeo's apothecary or some sly,
choice villain of Dickens'.

The ease with which Mary fell into Gifford's trap would
be incredible, if it were not for two facts well known to him
in advance. First was the royal prisoner's hunger for news
of the outside world, made all the more acute by the fact
that ever since leaving Shrewsbury's care she had been forbidden to write or receive any letters. And second was her
incorrigible trustfulness and belief in her ability to win
over even enemies to her cause. As early as 1579 she had been
aware that all her letters were passing "through the hands
of Walsingham," and five years later had warned de la
Mauvissière that the same official was trying to discover if
there were any secret means of communicating with her.
Yet later on she expressed her belief that he was "a plain,
downright man," who could probably be made her friend
if he really knew her. So when Nau, her secretary, suddenly
presented her with two letters at Chartley in the January of
1586, she seems to have felt nothing but a most childlike
joy. One was from Morgan in Paris, imprudently recom-
mending Gilbert Gifford; the other from Gifford, recom-
mending himself as a kind of super-mailman. He had, in
fact, evolved a highly ingenious process by which her letters
were to be inserted in a tube plugged into one of the beer
barrels regularly left by a certain "honest man" — duly
bribed for this new service — at Chartley. What Gifford
naturally failed to mention was that every letter sent to Mary
was first secretly copied, or if necessary decoded, by Phelippes
and given into Sir Amias' hands for transmission to Walsingham: while those she herself should dispatch followed the
same method in reverse. It all seemed so simple that even
Mary Stuart might have suspected had she not been so
famished for news of her own world — and had she not her-

self had so fatal a fondness for writing. But after she received a batch of letters which had been accumulating for a whole year at the French ambassador's in London, she could not be lured from the trap. Feverishly she began writing again to her French cousins, to Lord Claude Hamilton in Scotland, to the proud but sympathetic Don Bernardino de Mendoza who had been transferred by King Philip from London — where he had aroused Elizabeth's suspicions — to Paris. And it was most characteristic that Mary, who could never hold long even to just indignation, should hasten now to repudiate her natural but perhaps not quite just resentment against James. To the French ambassador in Scotland she wrote begging news of "the health and state of my son, towards whom my extreme affection as a mother has never failed." She asked, too, for a full-length portrait of the young king, "drawn from his own person." It may be that, had she lived a little longer, some understanding between mother and son might have been reached: for James, on receiving the message, confided to the ambassador that he would have "served her effectually" if he had had the means, but was kept half a prisoner himself.

Meanwhile Gilbert Gifford, as an expert *agent provocateur,* lost no time in gathering together both in London and Paris those who were most likely to forward a new conspiracy for the overthrow of Elizabeth and rescue of the Queen of Scots. One whom he soon drew into his net was the reckless but sincere John Ballard, an unattached and overimaginative priest ardently looking for the restoration of the Old Faith. Before long we find this Ballard reporting to Mendoza in Paris that the English Catholics had had new courage infused into them and were certain that "no time is so opportune as the present to shake off the oppression of the Queen and the yoke of heresy that weighs upon them." A few days later Mary herself received from one Charles

Paget, representing her friend Morgan — whom she had herself warned that he was under suspicion and should avoid "meddling" with dangerous matters — a most imprudent letter on the subject of Ballard. Evidently the latter, with the enthusiasm of the *idée fixe* and quite hypnotized by Gilbert Gifford's sly encouragement, was now reporting great quantities of Catholic nobles, especially from the "North parts" and the West country, willing to take up arms as soon as they were assured of "foreign help." He added that Leicester and many of the best English soldiers were abroad fighting in the Low Countries, with the people "much discontented with the oppression used towards them." To make matters even more incriminating, he assured Mary of the zeal of these men for her safety and release from her keeper's hands — giving the final information that the invading army of her rescuers would probably land at Newcastle or some other northern port. As a parting shot this Paget confessed that he had promised Mendoza not to write the Queen of Scots until matters were brought to "more certainty," but felt he should keep her in touch with the march of events!

Obviously there was nothing at all novel about this new plot. It followed the familiar program of its many predecessors, including an uprising of the English lords aided by the invading army from France and Spain, the dethronement and, if necessary, death of Elizabeth — with Mary of France and Scotland safely rescued and set as Catholic champion upon the English throne. Its details, and its complete impracticality, were known to Cecil, to Walsingham, even to Elizabeth — who, by their encouragement, might even be accused of being accessories! But as Gifford was ineligible because he could so easily be proved a royal agent and as Ballard inspired enthusiasm rather than confidence, the next important step was to find a suitable bellwether to lead the conspiratorial flock. It may have been Gifford or it may have been Ballard who first decided upon the twenty-five-year-old Anthony Babington, for both seem to have known him either in Paris or London. His family, which was both honorable and wealthy, had come originally from Northumberland, but he was now living in a quiet corner of London — interested in his little daughter and his books, zealous in his devotion to the Old Faith and rather a leader of the chafing young Catholic gentry. He had long had a chivalrous allegiance to the Queen of Scots, too; and while they had evidently never met, he had transmitted some of her French mail during the imprisonment at Sheffield. To persuade this ardent and Quixotic young man to become leader of the ready-made plot which has ever since borne his name was not difficult. By early June, Babington gathered in his lodgings at Herne's Rents the disguised and not too sane Father Ballard, the poet Chidiock Tichborne, the soldier John Savage, and a few other zealots, along with the archtraitor Gilbert Gifford; and all took a solemn vow to carry through the project or see their lives "happily lost in the execution thereof." As everybody knows now, the project was quite unworkable, and its chief results were to bring Mary Stuart to the block and subsequently to unite Englishmen of all faiths by the threat of the Spanish Armada. But the question goes far deeper than that. Whatever one may think of the mistaken idealism of these young men — or of their commandolike methods of dealing with a desperate situation — the purity of their intention is above dispute. The Scottish Queen became a symbol of their devotion to England and to God. And when this devotion was soon tried by the bloody tests of torture and death, it did not fail.

It was in early July that Anthony Babington, evidently assured by Gifford of the complete safety of its transmission, sent to his "dread sovereign lady and Queen" at Chartley one of the most wildly reckless letters in history. As the blueprint of a proposed *coup d'état* is was entirely negligible, being founded on that old, imaginary allegiance of the Catholic powers of Europe, all working in unison and consumed with zeal for the rescue of Mary Stuart and the restoration of the Faith in England and Scotland! But as a revelation of Babington's own psychology and the psychology of his time its value is great. For it shows in action a son of the old gentry and the old Faith, on the point of leaving his fatherland through disenchantment at the "wretched and miserable state" of Elizabethan life; but changing his entire plans upon hearing Ballard's story of the great preparations of the "Christian princes" to invade England and save Mary. With a kind of mystical exaltation he writes of this new crusade which was to deliver "our country, far than our lives more dear to us," and offer a "last hope to recover the faith of our forefathers." And taking for granted the success of the native uprising and the help from abroad, he enters into dangerous details of the "great and noble action" upon which might depend the whole future of England as well as Mary Stuart; how he himself, with ten gentlemen and a hundred followers, would undertake to deliver her from her Puritan jailor — while six other gentlemen had sworn themselves to the "tragical execution" or "despatch of the usurper" (Elizabeth!). Then, rather naïvely, he asks the imprisoned Queen of Scots to advise upon military leaders, ports of arrival for the foreign troops, and other points upon which her knowledge must have been nebulous.

To Mary it was thrillingly exciting to receive a letter so full of hope and of self-sacrificing devotion. Yet, after all, she had had some experience with Norfolk and Northumberland. Her secretary Nau, although not too perfect in his allegiance, begged his royal mistress not to answer Babington's epistle. But it was not in her nature to hold back from an adventure which promised so much and could not, she thought, bring consequences much worse than her actual misery and impotence. So within a few days she was dictating to Nau a letter almost as imprudent if not as emotional as Babington's own. As these pages were cast into cipher by her Scottish secretary Curll, to come down to us not only decoded but tampered with by Phelippes, they lack the eloquent charm and clarity of Mary's firsthand correspondence. In fact she later repudiated their present form almost *in toto*. But they reveal the Queen of Scots as frankly exalted by the role of Catholic champion offered her, and willing to take large chances to play it out. To be sure, she does warn the "trusty and well beloved" Babington against sharing his plans with too many people, even those who were or pretended to be clerics; and against hasty action before he was well assured of sufficient help from the foreign princes. And she advises him to consult with her Spanish champion, de Mendoza, in Paris (to whom she herself soon wrote a series of dangerous letters outlining the conspiracy for her release). But on the whole she was full of hope: offering some rather practical suggestions about the means of rescuing her from Poulet's care, and declaring her wish to reward Babington and his friends as generously as she should ever be able. "Whatsoever issue the matter taketh," she concludes, "I do and will think myself obliged, as long as I live, towards you for the offers you make to hazard yourself as you do for my delivery."

It is notable that throughout Mary Stuart's own trial a few months later she protested that while she had appealed repeatedly for rescue from abroad and naturally promised to reward those who should accomplish that longed-for liberation, she never encouraged or entered into any plans for Elizabeth's death. This is borne out by her reply to Babington, in which she warns that if his project for a large-scale uprising fails, her case with the English Queen will probably be worse than ever. Several disputed and contradictory passages — especially the postscript categorically demanding the names of the "six gentlemen" who were supposed to despatch Elizabeth *before* Mary's rescue — bear every evidence of being interpolations forged by Phelippes to further Walsingham's espionage activities. But such as it was, the letter was enough to incriminate the Queen of Scots; and on the copy transmitted to Walsingham, Phelippes had ironically sketched a gallows by way of comment. Gilbert Gifford's plot had succeeded.

After a short period of waiting, Phelippes inquired of his mastermind, Walsingham, whether Babington was now to be "apprehended or otherwise played with"; and as the latter's second letter gave no further revelations — for the reason that there were no more to give — the Powers That Be decided that the time for a wholesale apprenhension had come. Anthony Babington and his close associates were captured, tortured, and on September 26th executed at St. Giles in the Fields with unspeakable barbarity. It is thought that some of the more gruesome details were protested by the foreign ambassadors in London, for when the remainder of the group were put to death shortly afterward it was with less sickening cruelty. Meanwhile, of course, Gifford, the instigator of the plot, was allowed to escape to France — where he continued his career as spy, sacrilegiously received Holy Orders to facilitate his work, and eventually died in prison.

Mary had no way of knowing even of the arrests as yet, and was pleasantly surprised when her jailor, Sir Amias, invited her early in August to take part in a stag hunt at the neighboring estate of Tixall. Delighted to mount a horse again even in spite of her rheumatism, she accepted with her usual absence of suspicion. But before they had ridden far they were met by a royal messenger, who announced that Queen Elizabeth thought it "very strange" that in view of all her kindnesses, the Queen of Scots was conspiring against her. Mary denied the charge, and called to her secretary, Nau, for consultation: but both he and Curll were hurried away and taken into custody. Soon she realized that she was being pushed on to Tixall not as a guest but as a prisoner. For nine days she was held there *incommunicado,* while her desks at Chartley were rifled by Walsingham's agent of all her most private papers and ciphers. When she returned she must have realized at once the new and acute peril of her situation. And pathos is added to the tragedy by the story of her awaking in the night to find Sir Amias Poulet carefully extracting from her escritoire some small savings she had put aside for the expenses of her funeral and her few remaining servants.

She had not long to wait or wonder. Before September was out Mary was removed to the sinister and impregnable keep of Fotheringay Castle in Northamptonshire. This final station of her Via Crucis is one no pilgrim can visit today. For in a fit of shamed remorse her son ordered it razed to the ground when, after Elizabeth's death, he became James I of England.

CHAPTER   XXV

FOTHERINGAY

I T WAS soon evident that at Fotheringay the
Queen of Scots was to be tried for her life on a charge of
high treason against the Queen of England. It was evident,
also, that she was to be condemned: for Cecil, Walsingham,
and Company were convinced "that devilish woman" and
symbol of English Catholicism had become a peril to Elizabeth and all her "faithful servants." Poulet, the Puritan
jailor who continued his guardianship over Mary's last
prison, soon appeared at her door craving an audience. What
he had to say was that his mistress, Queen Elizabeth, being
greatly surprised to hear that Mary denied the charges recently brought against her, was sending a choice group to
interrogate her. He added that if his prisoner would confess
her guilt and throw herself upon the mercy of the crown
it might be greatly to her advantage. This rather obvious
advice Mary summarily dismissed; adding with a fine blending of pride and humility that while she had committed
many offenses against God, whose pardon she continually
sought, she was not as a sovereign Queen conscious of any
fault which she had need to confess.

A few days later Sir Amias returned, accompanied by a
small vanguard of the half-hundred official bloodhounds already gathering in the castle and village of Fotheringay. The

four messengers handed her a letter bearing the royal seal of England, but addressed with characteristic Tudor churlishness simply "To the Scottish." It was a thoroughly crude and cruel epistle, the wording of which Mary herself attributed to her enemy Walsingham. However it bore the signature of Elizabeth, and announced that the latter had dispatched divers of her "chief and most ancient noblemen," with several members of the Privy Council, to whose questions Mary Stuart was "advised and required" to answer as to their Queen herself. If Mary had any doubt about the intention of this "inquiry" it was dissipated as she read the ominous assurance, in answer to her earlier protestation of innocence, that "the contrary will be verified and maintained against you." As a matter of fact all such doubts and hope, too, had gone. She understood at last both the intention and the outcome of the approaching trial, and the superb fight she had determined to put up seems to have been entirely a matter of principle.

After reading through the letter or arraignment she thought silently a few moments, and then began an answer notable for the clearness and the courtesy which were part of herself and her French upbringing. She was, she protested, grieved that her "dear sister Elizabeth" had been misinformed, as so often before; but for herself, she had foreseen after the Act of Association that she must bear the blame of "whatsoever danger should happen either from foreign princes abroad, or from ill-disposed people at home, or for religion's sake." For a moment she referred ruefully to her long and illegal imprisonment and to Elizabeth's secret dealings with young James. Then, coming to the letter, she expressed surprise that her English cousin should command her as a subject to appear in self-defense. One can almost see Mary of France and Scotland, broken in body but not in spirit, as she protested: "I am an absolute Queen, and will do nothing which may prejudice either my own majesty, or other princes, or my son." She added that while she was ignorant of the laws and statutes of England and had no counselor, nor even her own notes and papers, she was determined not to sink under her calamities.

Alone and unadvised, it is evident that she had already, by something very like legal genius, hit upon her dual line of defense. As an equal Queen, unjustly detained, she was not amenable to English laws. If forced, she would enter a plea of not guilty, throwing the entire burden of proof upon her accusers. But with something of the old proud, careless candor she admitted: "I cannot deny that I have commended myself and my cause to foreign princes."

To the crafty Cecil and Walsingham, who next arrived at Fotheringay, the indomitable dignity of the helpless woman they had hoped to bully was amazing and exasperating. Used as they were to the alternating tantrums and acquiescence of Elizabeth, they marveled at this captive Queen who refused to answer as an English subject — which she obviously was not — and who pointed out the invalidity in trying her by either canon or common law. The Lord Treasurer's blunt assertion that the inquiry would proceed whether she was present or not — and Lord Hatton's more gentle assurance that she would not compromise her royal rights by consenting to clear herself — finally brought Mary into the arena. But she would promise to answer *upon this point alone,* the life of Elizabeth; and insisted she was not to be charged but by her "own word or writing." "Search your consciences," she added, "look well to your honor, and may God reward you and yours for your judgment!"

On the morning of October 14th, Mary Stuart, limping slightly, was led by her steward, Andrew Melville, and her physician, Bourgoyne, into the great hall of Fotheringay which was to be her courtroom. At one end of the room

was a dais with a state canopy bearing the arms of England —
representing the absent Elizabeth — opposite it, a small chair
of red velvet for the prisoner. Automatically and a little
wearily Mary registered her protest that as a queen by birth
her place should be beneath the royal canopy. Then she took
the humble seat assigned her, facing the two Chief Justices,
Bromley the Lord Chancellor, and some fifty earls and
knights, including Cecil the mighty Lord Treasurer and her
old enemies Secretary Walsingham and Sir Amias Poulet.

"Alas," whispered Mary to her loyal but helpless Melville,
"here is a great number of councilors, yet not one of them
is for me!" It was quite true: for the final infamy of this
second mock trial was that she was allowed no defense
attorney at all.

When the Lord Chancellor had read his formal accusation, she rose to reiterate that she had come into England
under Elizabeth's promise of aid against her enemies at
home — which could be proved if she had her private papers
with her. Once again she cited her unjust imprisonment and
repeated that her consent to answer before the court was
not to be construed as any waiving of her queenly rights:
adding that she made this protestation not out of regard
for her life or to conceal the truth, but solely to protect the
royal prerogatives she was handing on to her successors.
"I am not guilty of this crime against the person of the
Queen, with which, it seems, I am charged. I wish to reply
to this point alone."

There followed a long and confused discussion of Babington and his plot, with the reading of letters said to have been
dictated by that hapless man "from memory" — and under
what circumstances can be imagined — before his execution.
There were also depositions from her imprisoned secretaries,
Nau — who is known now to have been receiving a pension
from Elizabeth — and his follower Curll. The Scottish

Queen, refusing at first to admit any of this evidence, demanded as she had every legal right to do, not secondhand copies but originals of her correspondence. "If my enemies possess them, why do they not produce them?" she asked unanswerably. But it was the old story of the Casket Letters again.

Being pressed about the passage in her alleged letter to Babington concerning the "six gentlemen" supposed to dispatch Elizabeth, Mary denied having written it and consequently knowing its meaning. Then, with fine daring, she herself took the role of accuser. "It is easy to imitate ciphers and handwriting," she declared. "I am afraid all this is the work of Monsieur de Walsingham for my destruction . . . who, I am certain, has tried to deprive me of my life and my son of his. . . . I would a hundred times rather have lost my life than to see so many Catholics suffer for my sake and be condemned to a cruel death through hatred of my person."

To this Cecil, Lord Burghley, had the audacity to reply that no faithful subject had been put to death in England for his religion, but only for treason. With the same Machiavellian casuistry Walsingham rose to protest that "as a private person" he had done "nothing unworthy of an honest man," and as Secretary of State "nothing unbefitting his duty."

Never, perhaps, had Mary Stuart shone with a more compelling magnificence than during this brief and one-sided trial. She protested that, ill as she obviously was, she had no wish to reign in England: yet to Cecil's badgering she did not hesitate to add, "I have never given up my rights. I do not now and never will." And she reminded the lords how the young Elizabeth, although quite innocent, had been accused of participating in Wyatt's plot against Mary Tudor.

On the second day Cecil, probably feeling that the prosecution was not making much progress, himself took over the cross-examination. There were more letters produced — copies, of course, never originals — and by this time the Queen of Scots willingly admitted certain parts of the epistles to Paget, Morgan, de Mendoza, and even Babington, but only those dealing with the project of her escape from prison. Demanding that Curll and Nau, her secretaries, be personally examined in her presence, she begged: "Show me at least the minutes of my correspondence . . . they will bear witness to what I assert." This direct plea of Mary's, together with a later one in which she begged that all the private papers stolen from her desk at Chartley be put into Elizabeth's own hands, are probably the strongest objective proof of her innocence. It is eloquent that both requests were ignored.

Finally even Mary's patience was exhausted, and she cried out: "With what injustice is this cause conducted against me! My letters are garbled and wrested from their true meaning — the originals kept from me." Protesting that no respect was shown either to the religion she professed and for which she was ready to shed her blood, or to her sacred eminence as Queen, and making one final appeal to be heard directly before Elizabeth and her Parliament, she rose and left the improvised courtroom. The scene following seems to have been one of general bedlam; but sentence would in any case have been held up, as a "secret countermand" had come from Elizabeth ordering the court's final meeting to be held in ten days at Westminster. That night Walsingham wrote to the Earl of Leicester that he feared her Majesty had "no power to proceed against . . . this wicked creature . . . as her own safety demanded." And to Elizabeth's secretary, Davison, Cecil himself reported Mary's protest "that the points of the letters that concerned the practice against the Queen's Majesty's person were never by her written nor of her knowledge; the rest, for invasion, for escaping by force, she said she would neither deny or affirm." He added that there was long and "great debate" among the judges after hearing her.

Quite evidently Elizabeth was unwilling to fall back upon the Act of Association — which, of course, could convict almost anybody — because of possible protests from France and Spain. And quite as evidently her Lord Treasurer and Secretary of State did not feel they had proved their case at Fotheringay. But the Star Chamber of Westminister was notoriously successful in smoothing out such legal difficulties. There, on October 25th, the Lords of the Council brought in a verdict of guilty — meaning a sentence of death — against Mary Stuart. One man alone persisted in his dissent, so earning a place on the records of human courage and integrity. This was Lord Zouche, who was never satisfied that Mary had "compassed, practiced or imagined Elizabeth's death." It seems likely that Cecil and his Queen were not satisfied, either; for within a few days the verdict was rather suspiciously bolstered up by a petition from Parliament that the death sentence against the Queen of Scots "be executed forthwith," lest the "heavy displeasure and punishment of the Almighty God" should fall upon a too lenient Elizabeth!

When news of the coming catastrophe was carried by two of the lords to Fotheringay, Mary received it not only with dignity but with a curious detachment. Throughout much of her long "fever called living" it is impossible not to feel that she walked before destiny with an almost somnambulistic helplessness. She had been a girl of charm and brilliance, a woman of compelling magnetism and mentality — and several times a queen to boot. Yet she was palpably and lamentably overinfluenced by Henri II and the Guise uncles in France; by Moray, Rizzio, Darnley and Bothwell in

Scotland; while the very injustice of her position in England made her the ready victim of such visionaries as Norfolk and Rudolphi, Ballard and Babington. And after each disillusion or frustration she had been likely to sink into the escape of a semihysterical collapse. All that was over now. Sometime during that lonely trial at Fotheringay Mary reached the moment when she was at last able to face reality — the reality of changeful man and a changeless God. *In my end is my beginning* was the device she had long ago chosen for her royal dais, just when or why nobody seems certain. As she was never a mystic, although often a poet, and could scarcely have foreseen the political paradox of the future, it is likeliest she had in mind simply the wistful hope of Christian immortality. Later she discovered that a thought is a thing and a seed dropped carelessly may spring into sudden flower. In her youth Mary had taken both her inherited queenhood and her inherited religion somewhat for granted. In the stormy middle years when both were attacked, she fought back bravely but ineffectually. It was in prison that she became a champion of the royal rights and a zealot for the Catholic Faith — and now, for the dual cause of both, she was quite ready to go to martyrdom. She had made her own that final, mysterious paradox of *the strength of the weak.*

Ironically enough, just as the cryptic motto with which she had lived so many years was bearing fruit of a new reality in Mary's life, it was torn from her sight. Henry III's ambassador in London wrote back to France of the "pitiable condition to which the Queen of Scots is reduced," adding that Sir Amias Poulet has taken away the royal dais from her room and caused her bedchamber to be hung with black "as for a dead woman." It is recounted that the petty Puritan jailor also insisted upon sitting down in the royal presence without removing his hat. But Mary's own reactions to this next-to-final ordeal are best revealed in a letter written to Elizabeth during the November following her sentence. It asks no pardon, no delay, but declares the captive Queen's resolution to strengthen herself "in Christ Jesus alone, who . . . never fails in His justice and consolation, especially to those who are bereft of all human aid" — and it asserts quite boldly Mary's understanding that she is to suffer death "for upholding the obedience and authority of the apostolical Roman Catholic Church." "Now, since I have been on your part informed of the sentence," she continues, "Lord Buckhurst and Beale having admonished me to prepare for the end of my long and weary pilgrimage, I beg to return you thanks on my part for these happy tidings. . . . I will accuse no one; nay, I pardon with a sincere heart everyone, even as I desire everyone may grant forgiveness to me, God the first." She has a few final and urgent requests: the return of her chaplain, who has been removed to another part of the castle when she needs him most; and of the small moneys which have been taken from her and with which she desires to reward her faithful servants. She is anxious that these latter may witness her death so there can be no charge of suicide, and that they be permitted to bury her body in holy ground, "with the other queens of France" — or at Rheims with her mother. And she supplicates Elizabeth for permission "to send a jewel and last adieu to my son, with my dying benediction." Finally and briefly Mary Stuart tells of the recent humiliations of her prison, adding: "After they had done all in their power to degrade me from my rank, they told me that I was but a mere dead woman, incapable of dignity. God be praised for all!"

This was the letter which, the Earl of Leicester confided to Walsingham, "wrought tears" from Elizabeth. But Elizabeth's tears were quickly overruled by expediency and the men about her.

L⌐⎾⎾⎾⎾⎾⎾⎾⎾⎾⎾⎾⎾⎾⎾⎾⎾⎾⎾⎾⎾⌐

CHAPTER XXVI

THE LAST ACT

MARY STUART, then, was quite ready to accept
martyrdom. But not knowing when it would come, she determined to go on with life as gracefully, even as matter-
of-factly as possible. She was surrounded in the fortress of
Fotheringay by her household of about a dozen persons:
Andrew Melville the steward or *maître d'hôtel,* De Préau
the aged French chaplain (when he was not spirited away by
Poulet's guards), Bourgoyne the devoted physician, an
apothecary, a cook, a few pages, and four maids and ladies-
in-waiting — including the gallant Jane Kennedy who had
followed her since Lochleven, but lacking now that childhood's friend, Mary Seaton, whom ill-health had forced to
leave the prison for a convent in Belgium. There was also
— and one wishes its name were known, so it could be repeated whenever the final tragedy is retold — at least one of
the adoring little dogs who had shared her captivity. So
Mary was not precisely lonely as she greeted her forty-fourth
birthday on December 8th, nor the greater Birthday on
December 25th. And through the gray days of January, in
spite of the crippling rheumatism which had become
chronic, she went on cheerfully with her reading, her embroidery — Poulet lists an "unfinished" piece with floss "of
all colors" among the modest jewels and ornaments found

in the rooms after her death — while there was even occasional music among the fellow captives.

Mary could not have known of several now historic letters being circulated during the first month of 1587. One of these was from her son, the impecunious young James VI of Scotland, complaining to Elizabeth that she had "taken so ill" his former pleas and protesting the death sentence passed against his mother. While far from personal, the letter contained one argument likely to carry weight: that it was a monstrous thing for sovereign princes themselves to give example in "the profaning of their own sacred diadems!" This was something Elizabeth herself had thought of and feared as a dynastic boomerang, since royal executions had become dangerously frequent under the Tudors. There can be no doubt that if Henry VIII had accustomed the English people to the beheading of queen-consorts, the final murder of the anointed Mary Stuart paved the way for the execution of her grandson, King Charles I.

Some such guilty apprehension was probably at the root of one of the English Queen's most hypocritical and dastardly acts. Shortly after receiving James's letter, she quietly signed the death warrant of the Queen of Scots, but ordered it put aside for the present. Then on February 1st, Walsingham and Elizabeth's own secretary, Davison, wrote jointly to Sir Amias Poulet that their Queen found a certain "lack of love . . . and zeal in her service" in the fact that he had not already "found out some way to shorten the life" of his prisoner. With the Act of Association to wipe away responsibility toward God and the world, she "took it unkindly" that he should continue to "cast the burden upon her, knowing . . . her indisposition to shed blood, especially of one of that sex and quality, and so near to her in blood as the said Queen is." When this preposterous suggestion was delivered to Sir Amias the next afternoon, he immediately sat down to write back his "bitterness of mind" that he had lived to see the day in which he was required by his sovereign "to do an act which God and the law forbiddeth." Bravely enough he offered to return his livings to her Majesty rather than obey this command. For evidently he was a man of literal virtues, who refused to become an assassin although he had not scrupled to be an accomplice in the trap of the Chartley correspondence. "God forbid that I should make so foul a shipwreck of my conscience" he told Secretary Walsingham, "or leave so great a blot to my poor posterity, to shed blood without law or warrant."

When this letter was shown to the Queen by her now fearful Davison, she flew into a truly Elizabethan rage. "I do not like the legal method, as upon me alone will fall all the responsibility," cried the true daughter of Henry and Anne Boleyn. So Davison, upon whom she was eventually to shift the responsibility for Mary's death, hastened off to report to Cecil. Probably in fear that he might have to answer to foreign governments for the Queen of Scots' private murder, the Lord Treasurer extracted her death warrant from his papers and dispatched the Earls of Shrewsbury and Kent to see that it was immediately executed — without further consulting the now hysterical Elizabeth.

It seems to have been toward evening on February 7th, as Mary Stuart, feeling even less well than usual, was sitting at the foot of her bed, that the two envoys of death arrived at Fotheringay. She allowed them to be admitted to her rooms; and it was Shrewsbury — her friendly but harassed jailor in the old days at Tutbury and Sheffield and Wingfield — who began with some emotion to declare his wish that another might have brought the message with which he and Kent were charged by their Queen. "It is," he continued, "to admonish you to prepare yourself to undergo the sentence of death pronounced against you."

He must have been relieved when Mary, with no sign of tears, replied, "I am thankful for such welcome news."

She added that she had been expecting it for eighteen years; then her memory fluttered back still further, recalling that she was "a Queen born and a Queen anointed," near relative to the Queen of England and great-granddaughter of Henry VII — and had had the honor to be the Queen of France. "Yet throughout my life I have experienced but misfortune," she mused, "and now I am glad that it has pleased God, by means of you, to take me away from so many troubles."

She added a few words about her love for God and the Catholic Church, and for England: then, laying her hand on the New Testament beside her, she reiterated that she had never desired nor attempted to bring about the death of Elizabeth. "We should have agreed very well had I been permitted to speak to her!" she insisted with a flash of her characteristic optimism. It may have been the truth. In fact, it may have been the very reason that Elizabeth's ministers were always afraid of a meeting of the Queens.

Mary Stuart next inquired when her execution was to take place, and Shrewsbury replied: "Tomorrow morning at eight o'clock."

The Queen was a little stunned. "The time," she said, "is very short."

With quiet dignity she asked whether there might be a brief delay, as it would be difficult to make her will without consulting papers and accounts which had been taken from her. Shrewsbury answered regretfully that he had no power to grant any delay. Mary then begged that she might see her chaplain, who had been removed to another part of the castle, and was again refused. But to the Earl of Kent, a bigot of the first water, this seemed a good opportunity to urge the Queen of Scots to turn to the "true religion" by consulting the Protestant Dean of Peterborough who was — somewhat suspiciously — already installed at Fotheringay. With incredible patience Mary replied that she was sufficiently instructed in her own faith and ready to shed her blood for it; that to please Shrewsbury she had, while in his care, listened for a whole Lent to able Protestant preachers, who had failed to convince her.

"Having lived until this day in the true faith I do not find it now the time to change," she protested. Once again she begged to see the priest whom Elizabeth had restored to her, and whose absence when she needed him most she called "cruel and inhuman and unworthy of Englishmen."

There was a little more controversial sparring with Kent; but it is significant that at this crucial moment there was no mention of treason or Babington. Finally the Earl, so drunk with fanaticism that he blurted out the truth of the matter, cried to Mary: "Your life will be the death of our religion; your death will be its life!"

So, then, it was really martyrdom. . . . Mary Stuart regarded him with a triumphant radiance. "I was far from considering myself worthy of such a death, but now," she replied, "I humbly receive it as a token of my admission among the elect servants of God."

Then the intruders were gone, and the Queen of Scots turned to comfort the heartbroken companions of her prison household. For some reason both De Préau the chaplain and Melville the steward had been temporarily removed from her presence, but to the remaining group Mary spoke tenderly: "My children, it is now no time to weep. . . . You should rather rejoice to see me on so fair a road to deliverance. . . . Jane Kennedy, did I not tell you this would happen?" she cried with that strange new joy which was taking possession of her — the joy of the martyr, which even the martyr's loved ones cannot share! "I knew they would never allow me to live, for I was too great an obstacle to their religion!"

Mary was quick to use the energy which pushed aside her physical weakness, but even in her exaltation she was very practical. She ordered supper to be hastened that she might put all her affairs in order, and in Melville's absence the collation was served by the sorrowing Bourgoyne. Before its finish the Queen drank the health of each of her retainers, who tried tearfully to drink hers likewise. Then they sank on their knees, begging pardon for any faults that might have marred their service; and replying gently, "With all my heart, my children," she added her own plea for pardon if they had found any harshness in her. Next, sitting down beside her cabinet, she began distributing among these devoted ones what was left of her belonging — a few rings and miniatures, a pair of flutes and velvet-bound music book, some pieces of silver plate, and the crimson bed hangings. Also she carefully counted over the remaining gold and silver coins which had not been filched from her French dowry; dividing them into little bags marked with each one's name.

At nine o'clock she asked for inkstand and quills, and set about the last letters of her career. One of these she evidently hoped might be smuggled out to De Préau, for she told him how she had besought his presence to make her confession and "receive from you my sacrament." Being refused, she wrote now a general confession of sorrow for all her sins, begging the old priest to watch and pray with her in spirit through her final night on earth; and adding somewhat mysteriously that she would hope to see him in the morning, "though in their presence," and receive his benediction. Another note carried final messages to her brother-in-law, Henry III of France.

Next, *"In the name of the Father, of the Son and of the*

Holy Ghost, Mary, by the grace of God Queen of Scotland
and Dowager of France . . . being on the point of death,"
began most meticulously to make her will, naming the
French King and the young Duke of Guise as executors. Affirming that she died in the Catholic, Apostolic, and Roman
faith, she begged that Masses be said for her soul at St. Denis
in Paris — where she still hoped to be buried — and at St.
Peter's at Rheims. She left 5000 francs to the Foundling
Hospital at Rheims, 2000 "to my scholars," alms to various
mendicants; and small legacies to the faithful "servants,"
who ranged from her ambassadors the Bishops of Ross and
Glasgow, to Bourgoyne, Melville, De Préau, Jane Kennedy,
Martin the cook — even to the secretaries Nau and Curll if
they should be exonerated of her betrayal at London.

Exhausted, Mary lay back on her bed while one of the
women gently bathed her swollen feet. When Jane Kennedy
was ready for the usual nightly reading of a saint's life, the
Queen asked that she choose the Penitent Thief. "In truth,"
she murmured humbly, "he was a great sinner, but not so
great as I have been. I wish to take him for my patron for
the time that remains to me."

For a few moments she lay with eyes closed. Then she rose
and spent most of the night in prayer at her prie-dieu with
its ivory crucifix, her women kneeling beside her. There is
a persistent English and Scottish tradition that for some
time before this the Pope, realizing Mary's perilous position, had permitted her to keep in reverent reservation a
consecrated Host: which viaticum she administered to herself
in the dark dawn of that ultimate morning of her life.*

————

* For reasons of necessary secrecy at the time, it remains impossible to
verify this tradition, which all men and women of good will must wish to
be true. The beautiful gold and *lapis* salt-cellar of French workmanship,
said to have served as pyx, has long been preserved by the Maxwell family
in Scotland, and was recently displayed at an Exhibition of Highland
Treasures.

Then she drowsed for a little while. And at six o'clock on Wednesday, February the 8th, she opened her eyes and announced to her attendants that she had but two hours to live.

Bourgoyne, the doctor, noticing her pallor as he entered the room, begged Mary to take a little bread and wine. She consented to this; then, with a cheerfulness and energy amazing to those about her, bade her women prepare her for the meeting with Death. It was to be the tremendous encounter between a Queen and an Angel — also the End which was to be a Beginning — and Mary Stuart's dramatic sense prompted her to dress for it "gorgeously, as she was wont to do upon festal days." In the official report of the execution sent to Cecil by one *"R. W."* — who was either Richard Wingfield or Richard Wigmore — we are told that the Queen of Scots, still tall of stature and now inclined to stoutness, wore a trained gown of printed black satin, its loose sleeves set with acorn buttons of jet and pearl, and undersleeves of purple. Her kirtle was also black; and hidden beneath all this — doubtless in order that the blood might be as little conspicious as possible — she wore a petticoat of crimson velvet with an upper body of crimson satin. She added her usual headdress of white lawn edged with lace, with a collar and long veil of the same. Mary's rosary with its golden cross was at her girdle, and about her neck a pomander chain and Agnus Dei. The old and strangely detailed account adds that the Queen wore shoes of Spanish leather, and outer stockings of worsted covered her white Jersey hose, because of the cold.

Mary and her household were again kneeling in prayer when the sheriff with his white wand came knocking at the door. She rose with the help of Bourgoyne, and carrying the crucifix from her prie-dieu went out into the hallway. Here she was met by the English commissioners, Shrewsbury and

Kent, and by her old friend and steward, Andrew Melville. The latter, who had not been allowed to see his Queen for several weeks, fell upon his knees and kissed her hand. When she charged him with messages to her son James, and bade him bear witness that she died a true woman to her religion and like a true Queen of Scotland and France, the man burst into tears, crying out that her death would be the "sorrowfullest message" he had ever carried. Mary, too, was shaken for a moment and tears came into her own eyes, but she insisted: "My good servant, thou hast cause rather to joy than to mourn. For now thou shalt see the end of Mary Stuart's troubles."

Suddenly she remembered a small debt owing to her absent secretary Curll, and turning to the two commissioners asked that it be paid; also that her "poor servants" might be allowed to keep the small gifts she had given them and to return safely to their homes. She also demanded eloquently that a few of her own people might witness and report her death. Kent demurred, as usual: but after conferring with Shrewsbury he consented to her choosing four men and two women. So it came to pass that Mary Stuart began her death march followed by Jane Kennedy and Elizabeth Curll, by Melville and Bourgoyne, by her apothecary "and one old man more." This last is generally believed to have been De Préau, coming in lay disguise to give his final secret blessing; for probably, in the morning's confusion, he had been able to rejoin the desolated little group of her household. There was another humbler but not less loving member of her family who managed to slip out, too, and follow the Queen all unnoticed into the great hall which had been her courtroom and was now to be her place of execution.

It was suitably draped in mourning. And in the huge fireplace logs were burning, where the assembled nobles — who with the soldiers numbered several hundred — could warm their hands if not their hearts. And now, again to quote Master "R. W.'s" report: "with unappalled countenance, without any terror of the place, the persons or the preparations," Mary came out of the entry of the hall and approached the scaffold, which was "two foot high and twelve foot broad, with rails round about, hanged and covered with black, with a low stool, a long fair cushion and a block also covered with black." She needed Sir Amias' help to mount the steps; and thanked him with her usual courtesy, adding that this service was the last she would ever require of him. Then she sat down upon the stool, Shrewsbury standing on her left and Kent on her right, while the commission for her execution was read aloud — ending with a general chorus of "God save the Queen." With growing wonder Cecil's reporter noted that through all this Mary listened "carelessly as if it did not concern her at all . . . nay, with so merry and cheerful a countenance as if it had been a pardon from her Majesty."

"Madame," asked the reluctant Shrewsbury, "you hear what we are commanded to do?"

It had all become very simple to Mary Stuart. They were to do their duty, she said, although she was not guilty of the crime imputed. She forgave them "with a good heart," as she hoped to be forgiven: for indeed she knew it was because of her Faith that she was to die. No one contradicted her. But the waiting Dean of Peterborough hastened to conjure the prisoner to turn from Popish errors and prepare to die in the true faith he represented. Presently, having heard enough, the Queen looked down from her scaffold "with great earnestness" upon the fanatic who insisted upon intruding into her few remaining moments. "Good Mr. Dean, trouble not yourself any more," she said calmly. "I was born in this religion, I have lived in this religion and I am resolved to die in this religion."

Much against his will, the Dean's further harangue was cut short by the Earl of Shrewsbury; who seems to have suggested a compromise by which the Protestant lords were to pray aloud with him, and Mary be left in peace to pray by herself. This she did, first in Latin and then in English: slipping down upon her knees from the stool to intercede for Christ's afflicted Church, for James her son, and for Elizabeth her cousin. Once again she forgave all her enemies, and kissing the crucifix in her hand, cried out: "Even as Thy arms, O Jesu Christ, were spread out upon the cross, so receive me into the arms of Thy mercy!"

Incredible as it seems, Kent could not even then resist badgering the Queen of Scots. "Leave such Popish trumperies and hold Christ in your heart," he advised bitterly.

But Mary replied with sweet reasonableness: "I cannot hold in my hand the representation of His sufferings but I must at the same time bear Him in my heart."

Knowing that her ordeal was reaching its climax she rose again to her feet. And when Bulle the executioner and his assistant knelt in their black gowns and masks to ask the usual pardon, she replied with more than the usual grace: "For I hope," she added confidently, "this death shall give an end to all my troubles." As they reached out to remove her veil and outer clothing she protested almost gaily that she had never had such grooms before, and called Jane Kennedy and Curll's stricken sister to help in the official disrobing. Even so Mary "made herself unready with a kind of gladness and smiling," as the old report reads.

"Do not cry, I have prayed for you," she said gently to her desolate women, kissing them and making over them the sign of the cross as she bade them join Melville in prayer for her long journey. The Queen of Scots was standing erect now in her scarlet underdress, while Jane pinned over her eyes the beautiful Corpus Christi cloth she had chosen that morning for the purpose. Then Mary Stuart knelt down "resolutely, without any token of fear," said aloud the psalm *In te, Domine, confido,* and laid her tired head upon the block. Over and again her lips kept murmuring quite audibly *In manus tuas, Domine, commendo spiritum meum....* They were her last words before the ax fell. But even Bulle was not used to taking the life of a Queen, and he worked so nervously that three strokes were necessary to complete the martyrdom. Finally he held the whitened head on high for all to see; while the Earl of Kent and the Dean of Peterborough were particularly loud in praying that God would save Elizabeth and so destroy all her enemies.

Then a strange thing, "diligently noted" by all, happened. For as the executioner reached for the jeweled garters which were part of his perquisite, he saw hiding beneath the Queen's skirts the little terrier which had somehow crept up the scaffold steps and now cowered close beside her; "nor would it move but by force, and then returned and lay between her head and shoulders." At length the tiny, protesting creature was carried away by one of the attendants to be washed, as was everything else "embrewed with her blood." For Kent seems to have had a superstitious fear of any relics being preserved. Perhaps he was beginning to fear something deeper still....

All these details of Mary Stuart's passing come down on the word of eyewitnesses; and there is little difference between the testimony of Bourgoyne, the friend who reported to the French ambassador, and the mysterious scribe who reported to his master Cecil. Apparently this latter witness was just a minor young politician, eager to make his way and win favor with Queen Elizabeth and her ministers. It is more than a little illuminating to trace the note of awe and reverence creeping into his words as he watched this woman — whom he had heard accused of all the deadly sins — going out into Eternity with the smile of a saint and the last cry of Christ upon her lips. Perhaps Master "R. W." would have been the first to salute her as Queen of Paradox.

ⅬⅬⅬⅬⅬⅬⅬⅬⅬⅬⅬⅬⅬⅬⅬⅬⅬⅬⅬⅬⅬⅬⅬⅬⅬⅬⅬ

EPILOGUE: OF SUCCESS AND FAILURE

To ELIZABETH, Mary's death was naturally a source of relief and rejoicing. But as the bonfires flamed and the church bells of London rang out to celebrate the passing of this treasonable daughter of Antichrist — Public Enemy Number One! — fear, also, tightened the heart of the English Queen. Cecil and Walsingham being too high to censure for the hurried execution of the death warrant, she dismissed Davison, her secretary, in disgrace. And a week after the official murder she wrote to young James about the "extreme dolour" which overwhelmed her for that *miserable accident* which, far contrary to her intention, had befallen! She also protested that he had not in the world "a more loving kinswoman," nor any that would "watch more carefully to preserve him and his state." James seems to have understood and held his peace. He was already Elizabeth's pensioner and she was about his only hope of holding the Scotch or succeeding to the English throne. So in spite of Border raids by a few loyal lords, Scottish protests were really negligible. But those which came from France — in spite of Henri's civil wars — and above all, those from the finally aroused Philip of Spain, became increasingly ominous.

So Elizabeth Tudor decided that Mary Stuart should at last and at least be granted an official funeral. Six months after the execution, the leaden casket bearing her body was carried in state from Fotheringay to the mourning-

draped cathedral of Peterborough; where, before a congregation of English peers and peeresses, the dean who had
tormented Mary's last moments intoned the Protestant service and the Queen of Scots was placed in a tomb close to
another royal martyr, Catherine of Aragon.

It was not until quarter of a century later, when James VI
of Scotland had long succeeded Elizabeth as James I of
England, that he removed his mother's body not to St. Denis
as she had prayed but to Westminster Abbey. There, today,
the two Queens lie quietly enough beneath their statued
tombs in the noble chapel of their forefather Henry VII.
They were two rather pitiable women, pitted against each
other by the ironies of history into posts of symbolic rivalry.
What Belloc calls the "Elizabethan myth" was what any modern journalist would probably describe as a champion
"success story." Elizabeth was the child of a tragically broken
home — a slightly abnormal Cinderella, branded as illegitimate by her royal father, raised unexpectedly to the English
throne and quite as unexpectedly passing on her name to an
era of national glory. Art and politics combined to exalt her.
She became the champion of the New Faith she scarcely believed in and the new nobility she could scarcely trust — of
all that the world called freedom and prosperity and progress. And from first to last she was afraid of life and terrified
of death.

Mary Stuart had quite as exaggerated a sense of royal
power and royal prerogatives as her "good cousin Elizabeth."
Otherwise she was a woman of strangely modern sensibilities
and modern tolerance, compelled to play out her role on a
Renaissance stage of violent passion and war and treachery.
To man's love she turned probably less often than Elizabeth
but more completely: and she was defeated once by death
and twice by betrayal. Her intensely loyal friends were nearly
always less potent than her intensely persistent enemies. It

was scarcely by her own choice that she became the oriflamme of embattled Catholicism in the north; and for awhile it seemed that her human mistakes and missteps and misjudgments might defeat the mission forced upon her. Mary of France and Scotland was a kind of feminine Hamlet — if Hamlet's faith had been as strong as his doubts — by every worldly standard the obvious failure. Her own country cast her out: the England where she sought shelter forced her into technical treason and put her to death as a criminal. Yet all these confused endings focused into a new beginning. Even the English succession for which she had waged her losing fight was handed peacefully to her weakling son at the nod of the dying Elizabeth.

Gloriana, with the thosuand gowns in her wardrobes and the myriad poets and soldiers and explorers who had ceased to interest her — huddled on the floor of her royal chamber, mumbling in terror and senility as Death finally faced her.

Mary, Queen of Paradox, despised and rejected by men, limping to martyrdom at Fotheringay with such "smiling cheer" that many have thought she achieved sainthood at the last. . . .

Most of us know on which side we would rather cast our lots in the Eternal Reckoning. For after all, nothing is more relative than failure — except success!

A PARTIAL BIBLIOGRAPHY

of works consulted in preparing *Queen of Paradox*. Volumes particularly interesting to the general reader are marked with an asterisk.

Bibliography of British History, Tudor Period. 1485–1603. Edited by Conyers Read

Calendar of State Papers Relating to Scotland and Mary Queen of Scots. 1547–1603

Cambridge Modern History, Vol. II

Catholic Encyclopedia

Dictionary of National Biography

Diurnal of Remarkable Occurrents that have Passed within the Country of Scotland since the death of King James IV till the Year MDLXXV

Encyclopedia Britannica

Foreign and Scottish Correspondence of Marie de Guise, Scottish History Society

Baring, Maurice, *In My End Is My Beginning*

*Belloc, Hilaire, *Characters of the Reformation*

Birkenhead, Lord, *The Trial of Mary Stuart*

Bordeaux, Paule Henry, *Marie Stuart*

Brodrick, James, S.J., *Progress of the Jesuits*

Brown, John, *Queen Mary's Child Garden*

Chalmers, George, *Life of Mary, Queen of Scots*

*Dakers, A., *The Tragic Queen*

Goodall, Walter, *An Examination of the Letters said to be written by Mary Queen of Scots to James Earl of Bothwell*

*Gorman, Herbert, *The Scottish Queen*

Henderson, T. F., *Mary Queen of Scots: Her Environment and Tragedy*

Herries, Lord, *Historical Memoirs of the Reign of Mary Queen of Scots*

Hume, Martin, *The Love Affairs of Mary Queen of Scots*

Knox, John, *History of the Reformation in Scotland*

Labanoff, Prince Alexander, *Letters, Instructions et Mémoirs de Marie Stuart* (7 vols.)

Lang, Andrew, *John Knox; The Mystery of Mary Stuart*

Lewis, D. B. Wyndham, *Ronsard*

*Lingard, John, *History of England* (Belloc edition)

Mahon, Major-General R. H., *The Tragedy of Kirk o' Fields*

Masson, Rosaline, *Edinburgh*

Maynard, Theodore, *Queen Elizabeth*

Melville, Sir James, *Memoirs*

Mumby, F. A., *The Fall of Mary Stuart*

*Parry, Sir Edward, *The Persecution of Mary Stewart*

Pastor, Ludwig von, *History of the Popes*, Vol. XVIII *et seq.*

*Pollen, John Hungerford, S.J., *Mary Queen of Scots and the Babington Plot*

Read, Conyers, *Mr. Secretary Walsingham; The Bardon Papers*

Steuart, A. Francis, *Seigneur Davie; The Trial of Mary Queen of Scots*

Stevenson, Joseph, S.J., *Mary Stuart: A Narrative of the First Eighteen Years of Her Life*

*Strickland, Agnes, *Letters of Mary Queen of Scots; Life of Mary Queen of Scots.*

Teulet, Alexandre, *Rélations Politiques de la France et de l'Espagne avec l'Ecosse*

MORE OF LESS FICTIONIZED:

*Anderson, Maxwell, *Mary of Scotland*

Criss, Mildred, *Mary Stuart, Young Queen of Scots*

Drinkwater, John, *Mary Stuart*

Gore-Browne, Robert, *Lord Bothwell*

Hewlett, Maurice, *The Queen's Quair*

Irwin, Margaret, *The Gay Galliard*

*Masefield, John, *End and Beginning*

Schiller, Friedrich von, *Maria Stuart*

Swinburne, A. C., *Bothwell; Chastelard; Mary Stuart*

Zweig, Stefan, *Mary, Queen of Scotland and the Isles*

INDEX